Crowd Surfing

CROWD SURFING

Surviving and thriving in the age of consumer empowerment

Martin Thomas and David Brain

A & C Black • London

First published in Great Britain 2008

A & C Black Publishers Ltd
38 Soho Square, London W1D 3HB
www.acblack.com

A CIP record for this book is available from the British Library.

ISBN: 9-781-408-10595-5

This book is produced using paper that is made from wood grown
in managed, sustainable forests. It is natural, renewable and
recyclable. The logging and manufacturing processes conform to the
environmental regulations of the country of origin.

Design by Fiona Pike, Pike Design, Winchester
Typeset by RefineCatch Ltd, Bungay, Suffolk
Printed in the United Kingdom by Caligraving

For Alison, Daniel and Louis
And for Suzy, Izzy and Zach

Contents

Authors' note

David Brain is European CEO of the global PR firm Edelman, which represents some of the companies mentioned in this book. Specifically, Edelman works, or has recently worked, for London 2012, Microsoft, Pfizer, Starbucks, Unilever and Wal-Mart. Martin Thomas has worked as a consultant for Bacardi (the owners of 42 Below) and was formerly Global Head of Communications Planning at Mediaedge:cia (MEC). However, the views expressed about all of these firms are entirely those of the authors.

Acknowledgements

All books are the product of collaboration and with a title such as *Crowd Surfing*, you will hardly be surprised to hear that we would like to thank a crowd of people for helping us get to this stage. Bob Pearson at Dell, Robin Spencer at Pfizer, Steve Clayton at Microsoft, Dion Nash at 42 Below, Mark Turrell at Imaginatik, Charles Courtier at MEC, Peter Walshe at Millward Brown, Jeff Jarvis, David Butter, Mike Kuczkowski, Robert Phillips, Jackie Cooper, Tim Kitchen, James Thellusson and Guy Lawrence provided quotes, advice, encouragement and ideas that we could, if not steal, then certainly recycle. Larry Page and Sergey Brin invented Google and so made the job of researching background articles and other interesting stuff so much easier. Richard and Dan Edelman continue to earn David's praises for keeping the firm he works for out of the hands of advertising executives and accountants. Hugh MacLeod deserves much credit for simply being Hugh. The team at A & C Black – Jonathan Glasspool, Lisa Carden – had faith in our half-baked idea and hopefully helped turn it into something readable. Emma Ratcliffe deserves a medal for coping with David. Finally, Alison and Suzie kept us on the straight and narrow, listened to our moaning and not once threatened us with divorce. This book is for all of you.

About the authors

Martin Thomas

Martin has run just about every type of marketing communications agency during the past 25 years. He began his career in public relations before moving into advertising, via sponsorship, entertainment marketing and new media. At the end of 2006 he decided to go out on his own with Snapper Communications, so named not because he likes fish, but because he was accused of getting 'snappy' in his last job, which he took as a sign to move on. He now spends his time consulting, training and writing for a number of major brand owners and agencies. He studied Modern History at Oxford University, is married with two children and believes he would have won a Welsh rugby cap, had it not been for a dodgy knee and a complete lack of ability.

David Brain

David has worked in PR, corporate communications and advertising for 26 years; a continual span broken only by a brief gullible 18 months when he 'did a dot-com'. He lived and worked in Asia-Pacific for seven years and is now based in London, where he runs the European operations of Edelman, one of the top three PR firms in the world and the only one that remains independent. He continues to consult with some of the world's top companies and their brands. He studied Literature and History at the Redlands University in California and graduated from the University of East Anglia in the UK. He is married to a New Zealander, has two children and follows Manchester City FC.

Chapter I
Introduction

> **Crowd surfing.** *The process in which a person is passed overhead from person to person during a concert, transferring the person from one part of the venue to another. The 'crowd surfer' is passed above everyone's heads, with everyone's hands supporting the person's weight. It is believed to have been invented by Iggy Pop.*
>
> **Wikipedia**[1]

There is a story, probably apocryphal, about an architect who designed a university campus. On the day of the grand opening, he was approached by the head of the university, who commented that 'the buildings look fantastic, but why haven't you put in any paths to connect them?' The architect smiled knowingly and replied, 'I will come back in six months to put in the paths, once I have seen how the students have chosen to walk between the buildings.' Rather than impose his own views of where the paths should go, or use some elaborate computer simulation model, he believed that an enlightened architect should respond to the behaviour of the crowd.

Welcome to the world of the crowd surfer: a world in which a new generation of business and political leaders has learned how to harness the energy, ideas and enthusiasm of today's empowered consumers. They are not manipulators, demagogues or mere populists.

[1] http://en.wikipedia.org, June 2008

They have been smart enough to recognise that people around the globe – emboldened and enthused by a new spirit of enquiry and self-expression, and powered by the Internet – have changed the rules of the game. They realise that letting go – giving their customers, partners, voters and employees a greater say in the way that their businesses operate – is, paradoxically, the most effective way to ensure a degree of control over their corporate or political destiny.

Acres of newsprint have been devoted to the subject of consumer empowerment. As far back as April 2005 *The Economist* claimed that the consumer was 'king', and *Time* magazine named 'the consumer' as its cover person for 2006 – a title usually bestowed on the world's great political or business leaders – claiming that the year wasn't shaped by the deeds of great men, but by 'community and collaboration on a scale never seen before'.

The collective intelligence of crowds has created new business models such as Google and Wikipedia, and has even been the subject of a best-selling business book, James Surowiecki's *The Wisdom of Crowds*[2], in which the author argues that 'a large group of diverse individuals will come up with better and more robust forecasts and make more intelligent decisions than the most skilled decision-maker'. The key word in this quote is 'diverse'. Surowiecki does not advocate the rule of the mob, but instead believes in the collective power of groups of independently-minded people, each of whom can offer different types of experience and capabilities. According to his viewpoint, it is the diversity in their levels of individual knowledge that makes the crowd work.

The business and political community has not been slow to pick up on this trend. Consumer empowerment is debated in boardrooms, marketing departments and political campaign offices. It is on the agenda of every marketing conference. For some business and political commentators it represents the dawning of a new age: a revolution in the way that companies and other institutions communicate and

[2] *The Wisdom of Crowds*, James Surowiecki (Little, Brown, 2004)

collaborate with their stakeholders. Don Tapscott and Anthony Williams are typical empowerment evangelists. In their book *Wikinomics*, which has become something of a bible for the collaboration movement, they make the bold claim that 'For individuals and small producers, this may be the birth of a new era, perhaps even a golden one, on a par with the Italian Renaissance or the rise of Athenian democracy.'[3]

This hyperbole is echoed by many political commentators, who see the ability of political leaders to harness consumer empowerment as a means of reviving the democratic process itself. Not surprisingly, Al Gore, everyone's favourite New Age politician and the man often credited with spearheading the growth of the Internet as a political tool, is a supporter of the 'Internet as saviour of democracy' thesis. In his book *The Assault on Reason*,[4] he writes: 'So the remedy for what ails our democracy is not simply better education (as important as that is) or civic education (as important as that can be), but the re-establishment of a genuine democratic discourse in which individuals can participate in a meaningful way – a conversation of democracy in which meritorious ideas and opinions from individuals do, in fact, evoke a meaningful response.

'Fortunately, the Internet has the potential to revitalize the role played by the people in our constitutional framework. It has extremely low entry barriers for individuals. It is the most interactive medium in history and the one with the greatest potential for connecting individuals to one another and to a universe of knowledge. It's a platform for pursuing the truth and the decentralized creation and distribution of ideas, in the same way that markets are a decentralized mechanism for the creation and distribution of goods and services. It's a platform, in other words, for reason.'

Our aim in writing this book is not to add yet more words to the debate about the causes of consumer empowerment or why companies and other institutions should embrace it. We may not buy into some of the hyperbole – that this represents the end of business and politics as

[3] *Wikinomics*, Don Tapscott and Anthony Williams (Atlantic Books, 2007)

[4] *The Assault on Reason*, Al Gore (Bloomsbury, 2007)

we know it – but we believe that the reality of consumer empowerment has become broadly embraced. In our many conversations with business and political leaders – and those advising them – we have yet to come across anyone who denies that it has major implications for the way that they communicate and work with customers, employees, voters or other important stakeholders. They have largely accepted the idea that relinquishing some control of the communications process – encouraging a dialogue rather than a monologue and providing the means to participate – allows them to earn the trust of customers, employees, shareholders, partners, and, in the case of politicians, the electorate.

Where they differ is in how they have approached the challenge. Some have been cautious, fearful of losing control: they are guilty of what Marshall McLuhan many decades ago described as 'trying to do today's job with yesterday's tools and yesterday's concepts'. Others appear comfortable with the idea of relinquishing control. These are our crowd surfers; the people that concur with racing driver Mario Andretti's maxim that 'if everything seems under control you're just not going fast enough'.[5] They are people such as Procter & Gamble's Chairman of the Board and Chief Executive Officer, A G Lafley, who describes how business leaders 'are operating in what is very much a "let go" world'. He points to the success of the company's website for teenage girls, BeingGirl.com, as a great illustration of the commercial benefits that can be achieved by letting go. 'It wouldn't be as popular if we just tried to tell consumers what they should do.'[6] We believe that others can learn from the experiences of people like Lafley – their successes and their mistakes.

One business that has recognised, after much pain, the value of becoming a crowd surfer is Dell. The company's eponymous leader, Michael Dell, now sees the value in taking an open and honest approach to criticism: 'We sell 40 million computers a year and unfortunately we aren't going to get them all right, and every time that happens it hurts,

[5] www.brainyquote.com

[6] Association of National Advertisers, September 2006

but you quickly realise that these conversations [about these things] are going to happen, whether that is at CNET.com or wherever, so let's have them happen at Dell.com and let's go do something about it. And let's get involved in conversations all around the world and let's shorten our reaction time and the ability to learn from this.'

We will chart Dell's journey on the road to becoming a crowd surfer and compare the very different approaches adopted by Microsoft and Apple; the latter, for all of its populist credentials, appears far less willing to embrace the crowd. We will also examine how pharmaceutical giant Pfizer has successfully tapped in to the talents of the internal crowd and how, conversely, Procter & Gamble has looked beyond its own research and development resources to harness the creative skills of people outside the corporation.

Some businesses have tried to fight the crowd, resorting to litigation in an attempt to hold back the tide of consumer empowerment. They remain in what grief counsellors would describe as a state of denial, hamstrung by an instinctive impulse, when facing complex challenges, to revert to tried and trusted methods, even when they are clearly no longer appropriate. We will show how these aggressive tactics, rather than mitigating the effects of the crowd, have proven to be highly counterproductive. There is certainly nothing wrong in trying to protect valuable intellectual property or preventing outsiders from damaging the reputation of a company. It is just that companies need to pick their legal battles more carefully and accept that they can't prevent every single trademark violation and silence every critic.

In this book we will also look beyond the world of business, analysing how politicians on both sides of the Atlantic have embraced the concept of consumer empowerment. In many cases, they have understood its implications far faster than their marketing peers. Despite the description of the Internet by one political commentator as 'the lawless frontier of politics, a place where student hackers, sociopaths and saboteurs lie in wait',[7] a new generation of politicians,

---

[7] Tom Baldwin, *Fear and Blogging on the Campaign Trail* (*The Times*, 29th December 2007)

such as Barack Obama, Nicolas Sarkozy and David Cameron, has used Web-based communication (especially social media) to transform their party's approach to political campaigning. And, in the case of Obama, to reignite the political enthusiasm of younger voters. We believe that many of the techniques they have adopted to encourage participation and make the electorate feel more involved in the political process could be applied equally to the world of business.

The new marketing communications mantras for politicians and business leaders alike are participation, collaboration and dialogue. We will explore what is driving this desire to participate, and analyse the role of informed individuals in shaping the behaviour of the crowd.

Becoming a crowd surfer is not without its challenges. The mood of the crowd is volatile, and we will show how even the smartest companies can struggle to satisfy the demands that it places on them. The crowd, often with the blogging community in the vanguard, is always highly suspicious and naturally cynical. It will spot quickly any examples of what it believes to be inconsistent or hypocritical behaviour or a lack of transparency in a corporation's dealings with its various stakeholders. We will show how even the smartest marketing teams have come unstuck.

The other major challenge to becoming a crowd surfer comes from within. By nature we are all control freaks: we don't like the feeling of being out of control, especially in our professional lives. Unfortunately, you can't become a crowd surfer without abdicating a degree of control, taking a few risks and leaving the professional comfort zone. We will examine what type of personality is best suited to becoming a crowd surfer. How do they cope with complexity? Are the behavioural skills most commonly associated with female managers likely to become even more important in the future: things like empathy, sensitivity and flexibility?

This is not a book about the wonders of new technology. Neither of us are what you could describe as technology geeks – our pre-teen children almost certainly know more about computers already than we ever will. But we have witnessed the impact that new communications technologies have had on corporate life, and fortunately we have had the opportunity to talk to many leading technology thinkers. They have provided us with an interesting perspective on the impact of future technological developments which we are able to share with you. Crowd surfers don't have to be technophiles, but they do need an understanding of how technology, both today and into the future, is likely to change the nature of their relationship with the crowd.

We both like to think of ourselves as pragmatic realists. Between us we have spent more than 40 years helping all sorts of companies and institutions respond to social, political and economic change. This has given us a useful perspective on the way that they work and the best way to change their behaviour. But above all, we think that the time is right for a sober assessment of what needs to be done to embrace consumer empowerment.

We are not 'open source' evangelists, who argue that the only way to work is by collaborating with the crowd, nor do we believe that all communication has to involve an open dialogue. All of the evidence indicates that collaborative business cultures are likely to be more successful, and that dialogue tends to be more effective than monologue, but the reality of running a business or political party is that you can't always surf the crowd. Equally, the success of Apple, under the self-proclaimed control freak Steve Jobs, provides us with a cautionary example of how ignoring demands for open and sustained dialogue does not necessarily damage a business's performance. We explore why Apple's unique business model allows it to ignore the need to crowd surf.

Crowd surfing does not mean abdicating all personal control, becoming subject to the whims and prejudices of the crowd. It is not simply a case of being a crowd pleaser or a populist – a criticism that is often thrown at politicians who cannot face making unpopular political decisions, even if they are the right ones. Leaders should continue to lead: to debate issues with the crowd, try to influence its opinion and, if necessary, take a contrary position. As Allan Leighton,

Chairman of Royal Mail and one of the most revered business leaders in the UK, reminds us: 'Sometimes doing the right thing is the hard thing; leadership isn't a popularity contest.'

Rather in the way that a highly skilled meeting facilitator can control the ebb and flow of debate during a meeting or workshop without appearing to do so, the crowd surfer can respond to and shape the wider discussion within the crowd. We will show how some businesses have even become what we describe as 'crowd leaders'. These businesses have chosen to align themselves with issues beyond their immediate corporate interests. Prepared to take a stand on sometimes controversial issues, even if these might alienate some of their stakeholders, they behave more like activist groups than traditional companies.

Above all, our aim in writing this book is to provide practical advice for anyone contemplating the challenges posed by the empowered consumer, based on the experiences of other businesses and institutions that have faced similar challenges. Forget the hyperbole and the exaggerated claims that this represents the end of business as we know it. It is an interesting challenge: sometimes difficult, and occasionally feeling close to impossible, but we believe that given the will, every institution can become a crowd surfer. And that becoming a crowd surfer will ultimately make them stronger and more successful.

> *Listen to me. Learn from me. I was not the best because I killed quickly. I was the best because the crowd loved me. Win the crowd and you will win your freedom.*
>
> Proximo, *Gladiator*, Dreamworks/MGM (2000)[8]

---

[8] Scriptwriter, David Franzoni

Chapter 2
The World Seems Out of Control

> *All of the big changes that emergent technologies bring us are, for the most part, completely unanticipated by the people who introduce those technologies. It's out of control by its very nature, and if you could control it, it wouldn't work.*
>
> **William Gibson,** science fiction novelist and inventor of the word 'cyberspace'

To many business leaders, the world seems out of control: the level of public scrutiny of corporate behaviour is at an all-time high; criticism of what is perceived as corporate malpractice can spread at startling speed; domestic business issues can suddenly gain a global dimension; governments are rushed into anti-corporate legislation at the merest hint of a consumer protest; confidential internal memos are published online almost before they have left the CEO's office; employee disputes are being fought out on social video sites; potential new customers can investigate the opinions of previous customers, circumventing the blandishments of the glossy brochure or new advertising campaign. As a travel agent was heard to remark, 'I can't sell bad hotels any more, because all my customers check them out on Expedia before they pay me a deposit'. This isn't the way it was supposed to be.

One leader who can certainly empathise with this sentiment is Lord Sebastian Coe, former Olympic champion and now chairman of the London Organising Committee for the Olympic Games. On 6th June

2007, he and his team unveiled the new logo for the London Games and were met with a howl of protest. Within 24 hours, almost 50,000 people had signed an online petition protesting about the logo. Every amateur marketing and design expert seemed to have a view on its merits; it dominated the news channels for days. We will explore what made the crowd react in this way and analyse the effectiveness of Coe's response.

We will also highlight the problems faced by those businesses who have tried to hold back the tide of consumer empowerment through legal action. Their actions may have been correct from a legal standpoint, but they were completely counterproductive. In the online world, freedom of speech is considered by many of its most vociferous constituents to be a fundamental right, and any attempts to compromise this freedom are treated as an attack on the online community as a whole.

The companies who have resorted to legal action would have been better off listening to the wise words of online journalist Jeff Jarvis, who advocates learning to 'love the customer who hates you'. Like Jarvis, it is our belief that the most robust businesses should be capable of withstanding criticism from their customers; in fact, if they are smart, they should treat it as the most valuable form of feedback.

At the Mercy of the Crowd

Crowds are always unpredictable and mercurial. They can generate enormous feelings of well-being and shared identity; equally, they can be enormously destructive and irrational. Crowds are 'contested' and, to those interested in maintaining order, dangerous and scary.

Mark Earls[1]

Paul English is the type of intelligent, motivated and well-connected individual who makes business leaders feel out of control. This

---

[1] *Advertising to the Herd*, Mark Earls (MRS, 2003)

US-based blogger should be a hero to all of us who have spent hours lost in the twilight zone of corporate telephone systems, those interactive, multiple-option telephone systems that stop us talking to a real person. Paul created www.gethuman.com, an online directory, or what he described as a 'cheat sheet', explaining the numbers you need to dial in order to beat the automated systems and talk to a real person. Predictably, the corporations on Paul's sheet tried to put a stop to this heresy, but according to Paul, 'When companies change their interactive voice response systems as a response to the cheat sheet, their employees often tell me the new numbers and codes.'

The failure of some of the world's most powerful corporations to control a lone activist such as Paul English, or the behaviour of their own employees, who helped him beat the automated systems, tells us all we need to know about how the balance of power has shifted in favour of the consumer. It has led to a sense of helplessness in many of the world's boardrooms, which is summed up by Kevin Roberts, Chief Executive of advertising agency Saatchi & Saatchi: 'For the first time the consumer is boss, which is fascinatingly frightening, scary and terrifying, because everything we used to do, everything we used to know, will no longer work.'[2]

He exaggerates his point for effect. Not everything we knew before the rise of the empowered consumer has become redundant, nor every marketing technique thrown on the scrapheap. Consumers may enjoy a greater degree of access to information than ever before and feel as though they have more influence over the behaviour of their political masters and the suppliers of products and services, but their core beliefs, values and needs are not that dissimilar to those of previous generations. Whenever one comes across any hyperbole in the marketing communications world, it always pays to read the wise words of Jeremy Bullmore, advertising commentator and former Chair of both J Walter Thompson and the Advertising Association: 'I haven't read them all of course, so I may be wrong. But I believe it to be the case

[2] Quoted in *The Economist* (2nd April 2005)

that every single marketing strategy written since 1955 contains the sentence "It is essential that we recognise the increasing sophistication of consumers"...It's a puzzling form of self-deception, this. Comparisons across time are meaningless.'[3]

Despite Bullmore's words of caution ringing in our ears, it is possible to sense that, at the very least, there has been a power shift in favour of consumers and away from the previously monolithic corporations. The Internet has clearly been a driving force behind this change. To prove the point, Forrester Research undertook a simple Google search on the world's 20 largest brands. This revealed that fewer than 20 per cent of search results are linked to the companies themselves. About half are related to experts, the media and other sources. The remaining – and growing – 26 per cent come from consumer-generated sources such as blogs and product reviews, all of which are playing an increasing role in what the public learns and thinks about companies and their products.[4]

In a separate study of young Americans, Wikipedia was identified as the second most credible source of information about a company and, conversely, corporate advertising was deemed the least credible source[5]. The implications of these studies are pretty startling: the vast majority of the information about a brand's products and services online is not directly controlled by the owners or managers of the brand. It is a thought that terrifies many brand managers who have spent years deluding themselves that they are the ones in control.

We only have to cast our minds back to the millennium and the launch of Naomi Klein's *No Logo* to see how things have changed in such a relatively short period of time. This manifesto of the anti-globalisation movement depicted a world in which consumers were under the thrall of global brand owners. Consumer freedoms were under attack; global brands were too powerful, too controlling. She talked about how 'in ways both insidious and overt, this corporate obsession

[3] *More Bullmore: Behind the Scenes in Advertising* III (WARC, 2003)

[4] Forrester Research (2007)

[5] Edelman Trust Barometer 2008

with brand identity is waging a war on public and individual space: on public institutions such as schools, on youthful identities, on the concept of nationality and on the possibilities for unmarketed space.'[6]

She saw the consumer as a victim of this corporate obsession with branding: 'That we live a sponsored life is now a truism, and it's a pretty safe bet that as spending on advertising continues to rise, we roaches will be treated to even more of these ingenious gimmicks, making it ever more difficult and more seemingly pointless to muster even an ounce of outrage.'[7] It was a view that, at the time, pandered to many people's suspicions of the major corporations, based on a paranoid image of Machiavellian branding gurus, who wouldn't rest until there was a branded coffee shop on every corner and a pair of Nike trainers on every foot, inevitably manufactured in sweatshop conditions by an army of malnourished children.

It is an image of the world that, in hindsight, almost seems charming in its naivety. Far from being all too powerful, the 21st century has seen a weakening of the power and influence of global brand owners in the face of a rising tide of consumer activism and empowerment. Most of the global brands criticised by Klein have experienced difficulties. Nike has been forced on to the back foot by critics of its Third World labour policies; Howard Schultz, the chairman of Starbucks, has talked about 'the watering down of the Starbucks experience and what some might call the commoditization of our brand'[8]; even Coca-Cola appears to have lost some of its fizz, with a host of new product launches struggling to revive sales in its US home market. Consumer trust in corporations as a whole is at an all-time low.

Endless hours are wasted by people sitting around boardroom tables trying to second-guess the behaviour of what appear to be increasingly irrational and unpredictable customers. In a poll of UK-based marketers, 64 per cent agreed that it is becoming more difficult to communicate

[6] Naomi Klein, *No Logo* (Harper Collins, 2001)

[7] as above

[8] Howard Schultz internal memo (14th February 2007)

with consumers than ever before[9]. The remaining 36 per cent were probably too depressed to answer the question. Professor Stephen Brown of Cranfield University captured the pessimistic mood of the new millennium in his public address at the launch of Cranfield's New Marketing Research Group: 'The certainties of consumer expectations, behaviour, segmentation and communications that have underpinned marketing seem to have evaporated. Marketers are struggling to come to terms with splintering social structures, changing tastes and a fragmenting mediascape.'

One empirical study which gives an indication of some of the changes that have occurred in recent years is the Edelman Trust Barometer, which asks opinion-formers – essentially reasonably well-off, 35 to 64 year olds around the world – about who and what they trust. The study has for eight years asked the question 'Who do you trust as a credible source of information?' In 2005 a noticeable shift in attitudes became evident, with the respondents preferring independent figures of authority such as economic analysts or experts to established figures of authority such as a company CEO. A year later, a further shift took place with 'a person like me' becoming the most trusted source. By the 2007 study, not only was 'a person like me' confirmed as the most credible spokesperson, but a company's CEO had dropped to number seven in the list.

But who is 'a person like me'? According to the Edelman study, it is certainly not someone from the same demographic background, but rather someone who 'shares my interests' (61 per cent) or holds 'similar political beliefs' (67 per cent). Other important criteria are 'from the same community' or 'from the same profession'. This is probably intuitive. If we are going to trust someone's view or judgement, we are more likely to do so if they sound like us and have a similar perspective. The more 'like me' the person, the more likely we are to trust them and to take a lead from them. The crowd is certainly not undiscriminating.

These findings have been confirmed by a host of other research studies, all of which emphasise continually the importance we all place

---

[9] IPA, ISBA, MCCA, PRCA study (February 2007)

on the advice of friends and colleagues, or even the views of our fellow consumers. The force behind this growth in trust in 'a person like me' is the Internet, which allows us, through the miracle of search, to find people who share our particular experiences or interests. We no longer need to rely on what you could describe as official sources – corporate statements, political manifestos, media announcements – to provide us with information on products, companies and politicians. Whether buying a book, a holiday or a new car, the opinions of our fellow consumers appear to carry as much, if not more weight than those of the established order.

Perhaps the best example of this new order in action is in the relationship between doctors and their patients. A generation ago, a trip to the doctor was a hugely important event, treated with a kind of reverence. The doctor was a figure of respect and authority in just about every country and community in which he or she worked. Their stature was buttressed by years of learning and consolidated into the social and class systems at a very high level. In contrast, patients, even 20 years ago, were relatively uninformed and happy to defer to the medical experts. They rarely questioned the diagnosis or prescriptions of the almighty man (it was invariably a man in those days) in the white coat.

Compare this to the fate of today's doctor, who looks up to see yet another patient advancing across the surgery with a fistful of print-outs from a variety of very up-to-date websites and patient forums. Many of us have diagnosed our illness and even have a view on what sort of prescription we want, and even what brand of drug before we enter the consulting room. The dilemma for the doctor is very real, because medical science is a huge area, and a well-researched patient may well have more up-to-date information than GPs can recall from their memory of their medical training many years ago. And knowledge breeds confidence, and so the patient with the print-outs is much less likely to sit there mute as their parents may have done, and much more likely to question and challenge. Now, here some perspective is required. The 'wisdom of the crowds' can indeed be a powerful thing, but most people do not actually believe that, armed with a PC and a broadband connection, they are equipped to diagnose their illness accurately and safely and prescribe the correct treatment for themselves (though some probably do). What most people do want, though, is a proper conversation and to be treated much more like an equal in that conversation. The supplicant has become a partner (even if a junior one) in the conversation.

It is almost impossible for any doctor today – given the complexity of medical science and plethora of information and opinion available and easily sourced on any condition, no matter how exotic – to claim a monopoly on wisdom, and to be fair, most do not. As is the case in all walks of life, respect, deference, loyalty and allegiance are no longer awarded purely on the basis on formal titles, roles, academic qualifications or social status. Authority in this new order has to be earned and earned again, and that requires a very different tone of conversation and a relationship predicated much more on equality and fairness. The smartest doctors understand this, as do the smarter CEOs, politicians and academics, although it has left many feeling unsure and insecure.

And when we feel insecure, our instinctive impulse is to try to impose order on what appears to be a chaotic situation. Business guru Tom Peters believes that: 'Leaders resort to the command and control model when they are scared. That is, scared as hell that followers will figure out that they (the leaders) don't have a clue as to what the hell is going on.'[10] Fear makes us more cautious, more controlling, less collaborative: in fact, we become the antithesis of the crowd surfer.

The crowd, with Web-enabled activists in the vanguard, can force even the most powerful corporations to reverse unpopular policies. According to self-appointed consumer champion and occasional US presidential candidate Ralph Nader: 'Most people think that you've got to reduce sales a lot, but if you reduce any company's sales from (between) two to five per cent you've won. Having said that, it is very hard to reduce a company's sales by five per cent because it takes a massive degree of organisation.'[11]

[10] Tom Peters, *Leadership* (Dorling Kindersley, 2005)

[11] *Co-op America* 1989

You certainly couldn't accuse the global activist community of a lack of organisation: whether it is encouraging companies to stop trading with the Burmese military regime, campaigning to abolish the fur trade, or encouraging companies to pursue more environmentally responsible policies, the roll-call of success is extremely impressive.

One of the most high-profile victories for the activist community was when it forced US agrichemical company Monsanto to withdraw plans for its genetically modified wheat. The company's army of lobbyists and scientific experts were no match for a coalition of farmers and environmental groups, especially once the activists had pressurised most of the world's leading food manufacturers into renouncing the use of GM ingredients. Greenpeace celebrated the decision as 'a hard-won victory for every environmental group, every consumer, every cyberactivist who has said "no" to genetically engineered foods'. Monsanto continues to struggle to compete with the anti-GM activists. One of the first acts of the newly appointed Sarkozy government in France was to bow to environmental pressure and ban a strain of GM maize which had previously been grown by French farmers.

Food appears to be a particularly emotive topic for the public at large. When the Mars confectionery business decided to change the recipe for its famous chocolate bar and include an animal product, it was met with howls of protest and a Web-based campaign in which vegetarians were encouraged to boycott all Mars products. The threat worked, and within days Mars had reversed its plans and issued a formal apology: 'It became very clear very quickly that we had made a mistake, for which I am sorry. There are three million vegetarians in the UK and not only did we disappoint them, but we upset a lot of the consumers.'[12]

Even the world's largest bank, HSBC, found itself incapable of withstanding the power of a new generation of hyper-connected consumers. In the UK it was forced into a humiliating U-turn over the imposition of overdraft charges to university graduates, in response to

[12] Fiona Dawson, Managing Director of Mars UK (May 2007)

a highly proficient online campaign orchestrated by student groups using the social networking site Facebook. One HSBC executive admitted that the company's lack of familiarity with the site had been a handicap: 'We would love to go on Facebook and we have been having a discussion around that, but it is uncharted territory.'[13] The fact that Facebook remained 'uncharted territory' for a business with the resources and marketing talent of HSBC tells you much about how companies are struggling to compete with activist groups when it comes to embracing the communications power of new media.

And HSBC is not alone: so-called 'consumer revenge websites' have been set up to criticise most of the financial services providers in the UK. These include consumeractiongroup.co.uk, which was set up by Mark Gander as a platform to express his anger with Lloyds TSB about the imposition of £150 of bank charges, which he considered unfair and illegal. He was staggered by what happened next: 'The site was originally set up out of revenge and disgust at Lloyds. I expected it to be a couple of hundred people ranting about their bank, but we now have more than a million hits each month and 175,000 members.'[14]

Gander's initiative has also proved highly effective. His claim that banks act unfairly in the way that they charge people for exceeding their overdraft limits, bounced cheques or missed payments has become the subject of an Office of Fair Trading test case. He is understandably proud of what he has achieved in unleashing what he describes as 'a bank charges revolution', and claims that his initiative has made 'banks and others realise that they cannot continue to use bullying tactics'.[15]

It is difficult to find a business that isn't under attack by at least one activist group. The following list of activist boycotts compiled by *Ethical Consumer* magazine provides a fascinating overview of the many ways that businesses are capable of upsetting different consumer groups (see opposite):

[13] Joe Garner, General Manager of HSBC UK, quoted in *The Times* (31st August 2007)

[14] Quoted in *The Times* (17th April 2008)

[15] Quoted in *The Times* (17th April 2008)

Ethical Consumer's List of UK Boycotts[16]

Business	Activist complaint	Lead activist organisation
3 Mobile	*Investments in Burma*	Burma Campaign
Adidas	*Use of kangaroo skin in manufacture of some boots*	Viva
Altria (formerly Philip Morris)	*Donations to the Republican Party*	boycottbush.net
Asda/Wal-Mart	*Donations to the Republican Party*	boycottbush.net
Bacardi	*Anti-Cuba lobbying*	Rock around the Blockade
Barclays	*Financing of Narmada Dam in India and Trans-Thai-Malay gas pipeline*	CorporateWatch
Body Shop	*Animal testing, human rights issues and discrimination following L'Oréal acquisition*	Boycott Body Shop, Naturewatch
Caterpillar	*Selling bulldozers to Israel*	War on Want
ChevronTexaco	*Dumping toxic waste in the Amazon and failing to clean it up*	www.chevrontoxico.com
Coca-Cola	*Repression of trades-union activity in Colombia and depletion of groundwater resources in India*	Colombian Solidarity Campaign, India Resource Centre
Colgate-Palmolive	*Animal testing*	BUAV
Daewoo International Corporation	*Gas projects off coast of Western Burma*	SCHWE Gas Movement
De Beers	*Support for Botswana government's attempts to forcibly remove Bushmen from ancestral lands to resettlement camps*	Survival International
Dolce & Gabbana	*Using a chimpanzee in an advert*	Animal Defenders International
Donna Karan	*Sweatshop conditions in suppliers' factories*	National Mobilisation Against Sweatshops
Enterprise Rent-a-Car	*Firing workers seeking to unionise its Boston facility*	International Brotherhood of Electrical Workers

[16] www.ethicalconsumer.org

Business	Activist complaint	Lead activist organisation
Esso	*Sabotaging international action on climate change and donating to George Bush*	www.stopesso.com
Iams (owned by Procter & Gamble)	*Animal testing*	Uncaged Campaign
Joseph Ltd	*Use of animal fur in clothing*	Campaign Against the Fur Trade
Junckers	*Selling flooring made from wood likely to come from Indonesian rainforests*	Environmental Investigation Agency
Kimberly-Clark	*Destroying ancient forests in North America to manufacture tissues*	Greenpeace
Lonely Planet Guides (owned by the BBC)	*Publishing travel guides to Burma*	Burma Campaign UK
L'Oréal	*Animal testing for cosmetics*	Naturewatch
Lucozade (owned by GlaxoSmithKline)	*Donations to Republican Party*	boycottbush.net
MBNA	*Donations to Republican Party*	boycottbush.net
Microsoft	*Donations to Republican Party*	boycottbush.net
Nestlé	*Marketing of baby milk formula*	Baby Milk Action
Nouvelle	*Use of wood pulp from virgin forests & provider of advice to George Bush on 'conservative environmentalism'*	Ethical Consumer magazine
Pakistan International Airlines	*Victimisation of aviation workers*	International Transport Workers' Federation
Peugeot	*Moving production from UK to France and low-cost Slovakia*	Amicus, T&G
Procter & Gamble	*Animal testing of cosmetics, household products and pet food*	BUAV
Reckitt Benckiser	*Animal testing of household goods*	BUAV
SAB Miller	*Major shareholder Philip Morris's donations to Republican Party*	boycottbush.net
SC Johnson	*Animal testing of household goods*	BUAV

Business	Activist complaint	Lead activist organisation
Shell	*Environmental impact of oil exploration on Ogoni people in Nigeria*	Movement for Survival of the Ogoni People
Starbucks	*Lack of fair terms for Ethiopian coffee growers*	Organic Consumers Association
Singapore Airlines	*Threats of Singapore government repression during IMF and World Bank meetings*	Friends of the Earth
Superdrug	*Parent company Cheung Kong Holdings' investments in Burma*	Burma Campaign
Suzuki	*Investments in Burma*	Burma Campaign
Tesco	*Invasion of privacy with use of radio frequency identification tags in products or packaging, and sale of live turtles, tortoises and frogs in their Chinese stores*	Consumers Against Supermarket Privacy Invasion and Numbering, Care for Wild International
Unilever	*Animal testing*	BUAV

If your company doesn't appear on this list, don't worry, its day will surely come. And if you still need convincing that the world seems to have gone mad – or at least appears to have gone mad in the eyes of many in the business community – you only have to consider the bizarre situation facing Unilever when it bought the socially aware ice-cream brand, Ben & Jerry's. As a condition of the deal, Unilever was obliged to donate five million dollars to anti-corporate campaign groups. Some of this money was subsequently passed on to anti-capitalist direct action group The Rukus Society, who used it to stage a boycott of Wal-Mart, one of Unilever's largest customers.

Activist groups are not the only people capable of forcing even the largest corporations to change their behaviour. Sometimes it simply takes a pissed-off individual armed with a camera-phone, Internet connection and some creative thinking. The theory used to be that an unhappy customer will tell around 10 other people about a poor experience. No one told Delta Airlines passenger Robert McKee that he could only complain to 10 people. McKee's video account of his seven-hour delay on a Delta flight, '6499, Seven Hours on the Tarmac' (not the most creative title but, rather like the title of the movie *Snakes on a Plane*, it doesn't leave any room for misinterpretation), has been viewed 300,000 times on YouTube and generated a prime-time slot on CBS news. It also worked. It was only after McKee's video went viral that Delta refunded some money to the passengers who endured the delay. Social networks magnify people's experiences, both good and bad, with the providers of goods and services. Who needs the telephone number of the customer complaints department – that probably won't answer your call in any case – when you have YouTube?

The internal crowd is also becoming bolder and smarter in its use of new technology. Australian airline Qantas recently found itself fighting a rearguard action in an employee dispute about service standards. The airline unions posted a campaigning clip on YouTube, which resulted in hundreds of protest e-mails and signed postcards from disgruntled passengers. Australian Services Union Assistant National Secretary Linda White is in no doubt about the power of YouTube: 'A picture's worth a thousand words, and we think it will get passed around a lot,' she said. 'We think people will empathise with it and, obviously, it's a way to get people to look at the website and tell Qantas what they think.'[17]

Internet-based campaigns are increasingly replacing walk-outs and strike action as the trades union movement's preferred form of direct action. Many of the tactics used by Qantas's opponents have been copied by trades union activists in other parts of the world. Britain's largest private-sector union, Unite, adopted search marketing techniques in a dispute about workers' rights with retailer Marks & Spencer. Anyone typing 'M&S' into Google was directed to an advertisement from Unite which criticised the retailer for failing to live up to its own ethical trading standards, alongside the usual search results. For an investment of a few hundred pounds, Unite was able to reach a wide audience – more than 15,300 hits were recorded before Google blocked the link – and generate considerable publicity for its cause.

[17] Quoted in *The Australian* (3rd October 2007)

Unite has also posted videos on YouTube to protest against factory closures and the transfer of jobs abroad. The union's Joint General Secretary, Tony Woodley, is in no doubt about the importance of the Internet to the modern trades union movement: 'The power of the Internet gives unions the potential to go beyond their membership and reach out directly to millions of people and influence consumers. For companies like M&S, their brand is everything. A concerted campaign against a company's behaviour can be a very effective addition to industrial action.'[18] It is interesting to see how the trades union movement has identified fears about damage to a brand's reputation as a potential weak spot in the corporate armoury. A threat to the brand appears to be a far more potent weapon in any industrial dispute than simply withholding labour.

One consumer group that has been particularly effective at changing corporate behaviour is mothers. For many mothers stuck at home with young children, the Internet has provided an invaluable connection with the outside world, or at least a world away from nappies, Teletubbies and plastic toys. The UK websites www.raisingkids.co.uk and www.mumsnet.co.uk have proven to be particularly effective expressions of parent power. Woolworths was forced recently to stop selling a range of bedroom furniture, inappropriately called Lolita, for young girls following a Web-based revolt by Britain's mothers. A Woolworths spokesperson admitted that literary appreciation was not something that the retailer necessarily looks for in its potential employees: 'What seems to have happened is the staff who run the website had never heard of Lolita and, to be honest, no one else here had either. We had to look it up on Wikipedia. But we certainly know who she is now.[19]'

Even this piece of incompetence pales in comparison with that of UK retail giant Tesco's decision to market a pole-dancing kit within the toys and games section of its website, a move that was rapidly and rightly reversed following a wave of Web-based protest. Some corporate leaders

[18] Quoted in the *Financial Times* (27th February 2008)

[19] Quoted in *The Times* (1st February 2008)

may claim that their businesses have been the victims of unfair public criticism – that the expectations placed upon them are unrealistic – but in the vast majority of cases consumers have simply highlighted just this type of corporate ineptitude.

The Web has accelerated the speed at which consumer protests can develop, but the causes of most of these protests – a failure to consider the consequences of corporate actions, a refusal to consult important stakeholders, the inability to apply a little common sense – have not changed in decades. Good managers have the skills to cope with unusual business, economic and social conditions. They have also come to terms with the brutal reality expressed by the authors of *The Cluetrain Manifesto*[20] that: 'There are no secrets. The networked market knows more than companies do about their own products. And whether the news is good or bad, they tell everyone.' Poor managers and poorly managed companies, operating in a state of denial, simply go under, washed away by the tide of public criticism.

Coe's Ultimate Olympic Challenge

> *We, the undersigned, call on the London Olympic Committee to scrap and change the ridiculous logo unveiled for the London 2012 Olympics.*
> Web petition launched on the day of the unveiling of the
> London Olympic logo. The petition attracted
> 48,614 signatures before it was closed.

Double Olympic gold medallist Sebastian Coe (now Lord Coe) has always been a popular figure in the UK. His reputation even survived a brief stint as a politician in the unpopular John Major government. He is a composed and confident media performer, with impeccable connections throughout the world of sport. He was the obvious

---

[20] *The Cluetrain Manifesto*, Rick Levine, Christopher Locke, D. Searls, David Weinberger (FT.com, 2001)

candidate to lead London's bid for the 2012 Olympic Games and, by all accounts, made a critical difference when it came to the final vote. In the summer of 2007, he was still basking in the glow of the successful bid when he unveiled the London 2012 logo.

Little could have prepared him for what happened next. Within days, an online petition calling for the scrapping of the London Olympic logo had gathered almost 50,000 signatures. It dominated the news headlines and became the favourite topic of conversation for the nation's bloggers. Every self-proclaimed marketing and design expert appeared to enter the debate, offering Coe the benefit of their experience and suggesting alternative designs. Olympic logos have a track record of attracting initial criticism, but the Web-based furore surrounding the London logo became a global phenomenon. It was claimed at the time that 350,000 unique visitors from 178 countries visited the website of LOCOG, the London Games organising committee.[21]

So why did a consummate media performer like Coe and a very experienced communications team (including one of the authors) fall foul of the crowd? He did, after all, employ many of the techniques adopted by the smartest crowd surfers. London's leading bloggers had been given exclusive pre-access to some of the promotional video footage for the new logo. Interactive design competitions were included on the London Olympics website. The logo itself was created by one of the world's leading design firms, Wolf Olins, a company which has extensive experience of coping with the public criticism that tends to greet the unveiling of every new corporate logo. Their work was launched at a star-studded celebrity event, to an apparently receptive gathering of journalists and opinion-formers. What could go wrong?

The winning of the right to stage the 2012 Olympics resulted in a brief moment of national joy in the UK on July 6th 2005. For once, political differences were put aside and even the many critics of London's bid appeared to be carried along by the positive mood. Unfortunately this was to last a mere 24 hours. The very next day, London experienced the worst

[21] FT.com (7th June 2007)

terrorist atrocity in its long history. Four bombs targeting the London transport system killed 51 people and injured hundreds. Not surprisingly, terrorism and security, not the winning of the right to stage the Games, became the subject du jour. All of the goodwill accompanying Olympic chief Jacques Rogge's announcement that London had won the bid for the 2012 Games had collapsed. Any positive energy had been dissipated.

In time-honoured British fashion, the budget and plans for the 2012 Olympic Games then became a political football. Those directly disadvantaged by the proposed transformation of East London began to mobilise and organise their own campaigns. Many of these people faced the prospect of having their property forcibly purchased and their businesses relocated to less favourable locations. Critics outside East London also had plenty to shout about: the Games would suck money out of the arts; they would go over budget and the British taxpayer or London residents would have to pay for it; public transport would grind to a halt with the millions coming to watch; the British couldn't possibly organise such a thing in time; it would be a cock-up and a national embarrassment, and who cares about the Olympics anyway?

And the final element was the British media, for whom the run-up to the Games gave both the opportunity to drape itself in patriotism one minute and write disaster stories the next. It was soap opera that would run for five years and would allow them to berate officials and humiliate politicians. Motivated and articulate opponents and a cynical media were able to focus on a simple target: the logo. Introducing into this toxic mix a design created explicitly to 'shock' and to force disaffected youth into a reappraisal of the Olympics was like igniting petrol.

A logo, according to Wikipedia, is a design for 'immediate recognition, inspiring trust, admiration, loyalty and an implied superiority'. Logos, by their nature, are simple to understand and very easy to form an opinion of. It's not like deciding whether a Volkswagen is a better car than a Ford, a process that requires a moderately complicated cognitive process and a degree of technical understanding before a strong view can be articulated. A logo invites an immediate response, often a visceral one. That's its job. And so in its reaction to the 2012 logo, the crowd had simply to decide themselves whether they 'liked' it or not. And most of them did not.

The brief given by Coe and his team to Wolff Olins was to create a logo for what they termed the 'Google generation'. Coe's successful pitch to the Olympic delegates gathered in Singapore had made much of London's ability to create an event that would connect with young people. The IOC's own research had started to show how younger generations were falling out of love with the Olympics: to them they appeared like a quaint anachronism, the antithesis of cool. The logo was therefore created for them: shocking, vivid and so very contemporary. It was a logo for the digital generation, which looked far better in its online form than it did in two-dimensional print.

As soon as the negative comments hit first the Internet and then the talk-back radio shows, a tidal wave of criticism, comment and plain invective was unleashed. Here was an opportunity to voice views on a subject where your perspective was as valid as anyone else's – we're all design experts at heart – and then add to these views any personal gripes about the staging of the 2012 Olympics in general. National newspapers ran competitions for their readers to create alternative designs, and soon a feeding frenzy began. And to add even more fuel to the inferno, the launch website for the logo included a video that broke the rules on strobe lighting effects, creating a set of visual images that could potentially trigger epileptic fits. So not only was the logo horrible to look at, in the eyes of many, but it could also make you ill.

So with the nation blowing a collective raspberry at the design and everyone responsible for it, what course of action should Coe take? One response would have been to submit to the will of the crowd and modify the design or even start again. A number of national newspapers and politicians were calling for a popular competition, and in some respects such a decision to back down might have won Coe plaudits for being responsive and flexible. Instead, his response was pretty unequivocal. He held his ground, displaying the stubbornness of someone who had been used to winning battles on the athletics track. In an interview with BBC Sport, he outlined his case: 'It won't be to be everybody's taste immediately, but it's a brand that we genuinely believe can be hard working . . . and reach out and engage young people, which is our challenge over the next five years.'[22]

Crowd surfing does not mean always giving in to public pressure. James Surowiecki may have made a compelling case for the general 'wisdom of crowds', but the crowd is not always correct, especially when it comes to matters requiring aesthetic judgement. How many much-loved buildings or artworks were hated by the public when they were first unveiled? Equally, how many great works of art or truly imaginative designs were the product of a shared creative endeavour? Coe believed in the quality of the thinking that had gone into the development of the logo. He had faith in the expertise of the designers and the integrity of their solution, even if the wider public didn't like it.

Slowly but surely, Coe and his team took the heat out of the argument. Supporters of the logo design, including Olympic sponsors, leapt to its defence, as did Michael Payne, the IOC's former commercial director, who argued for a little more perspective: 'During two decades working at the IOC I learnt not to jump to conclusions on day one of a launch. London's brand will develop over time.'[23] The London team also took comfort from a document, originally produced by the people working on the Sydney Games, which, with tongue firmly in cheek, described the six-year cycle of an Olympic host city: 'Year one: euphoria; Year two: disenchantment; Year three: search for the guilty; Year four: persecution of the innocent; Year five: successful delivery and completion of event; Year six: glorification of the uninvolved.'[24] It is a cycle that anyone working on a major corporate initiative would be familiar with.

If nothing else, the logo controversy taught Coe and his team an important lesson about the behaviour of the crowd – the millions of UK residents and Olympics watchers around the world: if you want to do something dramatic or provocative, something to stimulate discussion,

[22] Quoted on www.bbc.co.uk/news (4th June 2007)

[23] *Daily Telegraph* (8th June 2007)

[24] Quoted by David Bond in the *Daily Telegraph* (8th June 2007)

don't be too surprised if the crowd takes you up on the offer. And as one of Coe's marketing team remarked, 'One of our tasks was to establish the new brand identity, without advertising support, so that it could be defended as a known trademark. At least no one could accuse us of failing to raise awareness of the logo.' For once, the adage that 'all publicity is good publicity' may be appropriate.

Trying to Hold Back the Tide

You would be wise to listen to the customers you're threatening to sue – they can leave you, especially if you give them motivation. Remember, they wouldn't be motivated unless your products were somehow missing the mark.

Jonathan Schwartz, Chief Executive Officer and President, Sun Microsystems, Inc.

American Jose Avila is both untidy and highly creative. Finding his house full of used FedEx cartons and being a bit short of cash, he came up with the radical idea of turning them into furniture. He started creating designs for his friends and, as word spread, he decided to market his alternative form of recycling on www.fedexfurniture.com. They are not the most beautiful designs in the world – there is only so much you can do with a FedEx carton – but they are certainly original.

How did FedEx respond to this fantastic PR opportunity that could only bolster their environmental credentials? Were the company's PR people smart enough to spot a great publicity opportunity, and sufficiently influential to convince the higher authorities within FedEx of the merits of Avila's project? Of course not. The FedEx lawyers were unleashed and told to shut down his site, claiming a breach of its copyrights and trademarks. Fortunately for lovers of the underdog, Avila was well-connected and able to enlist the help of some lawyer friends at Stanford Law School to help him in his fight. The results were all too predictable for those of us who have witnessed other corporate attempts to silence the little guys: Avila became the hero and FedEx was vilified in the media. It also missed a great opportunity to harness the creativity and enthusiasm of one of its consumers at no financial cost to its business. FedEx failed to crowd surf.

FedEx was following in the distant footsteps of McDonald's, which effectively created the template for how to completely over-react to consumer action and inadvertently create a situation in which the people with whom you have a problem become the heroes of the story. The McLibel trial took place two decades ago, but it continues to dog the company's reputation. Two Londoners, Helen Steel and Dave Morris, were accused of libelling McDonald's after distributing Greenpeace leaflets outside one of its restaurants, criticising many of the company's policies and practices. The leaflet was called *What's Wrong with McDonald's: Everything They Don't Want You to Know*, and included controversial claims about the exploitation of restaurant workers, damage to the environment, and promotion of unhealthy food that could lead to obesity and heart disease.

It turned into the longest-ever legal case in the UK, and although the verdict delivered in June 1997 went in favour of McDonald's, it was the hollowest of victories. The sanctimonious tone taken by *The Guardian* newspaper was typical: 'Not since Pyrrhus has a victor emerged so bedraggled. . . . Publicly, McDonald's, which has a notoriously unhealthy litigious appetite, has remained tight-lipped over its pursuit of two unemployed green campaigners with no assets, but someone somewhere in its empire must be asking some awkward questions. As PR fiascos go, this action takes the prize for ill-judged and disproportionate response to public criticism.'[25]

Two years later the Court of Appeal decreed that it was fair comment to say that McDonald's employees worldwide 'do badly in terms of pay and conditions', and true that 'if one eats enough McDonald's food, one's diet may well become high in fat etc., with the very real risk of heart disease.'[26]

[25] *The Guardian* (20th June 1997)

[26] Court of Appeal ruling (31st March 1999)

The so-called McLibel case became a cause célèbre for the international activist community and did serious damage to the company's reputation. It became the subject of a feature-length documentary, and is still used as a stick with which to beat the multinational corporations. Two decades later, *The Guardian* was still generating mileage from the case: 'In the 20 years since the London Greenpeace leaflets were first handed out, the debates about industrial food and corporations have grown enormously. The epic McLibel trial, it can now be seen, acted as a commentary on globalisation and helped to expose many of the dubious practices of giant corporations.'[27]

McDonald's does appear to have learned a lesson from the McLibel mess and has started showing signs of becoming a genuine crowd surfer. The company's response to yet another wave of negative press coverage in the wake of Morgan Spurlock's cult film documentary *Supersize Me* was to put a leash on the corporate lawyers and instead embark on an unprecedented campaign of public openness. The McDonald's website now includes complete nutritional information about every product, from cheeseburgers to milkshakes, and even includes a meal-tray calculator which tells customers how any chosen combination – such as a burger, chips and fizzy drink – must be balanced against other meals for a more complete diet.

McDonald's also encourages what it quaintly describes as 'civil dialogue' through its corporate responsibility blog 'Open for Discussion'. This provides customers and other interested parties with the opportunity to engage with senior McDonald's managers and 'gain personal perspectives on the issues, hear open assessments of the challenges we face, and engage in civil dialogue with the people behind the programmes at the Golden Arches.'[28] In one blog, they were even brave enough to upload footage from the site of a slaughterhouse: an image that you would not readily associate with Ronald McDonald, but proof that they were indeed ready for a free and open 'conversation'.

[27] *The Guardian* (15th February 2005)

[28] http://csr.blogs.mcdonalds.com

The company has also proven itself to be more adept at dealing with protest groups. When Greenpeace in the UK criticised McDonald's for its use, in animal feed, of soya grown in what had been rainforest, the company moved rapidly into listening mode. It placed a moratorium on buying soya from the areas it had deforested, and then tried to put its case to the campaigners. According to McDonald's UK Vice-president of Communications, Nick Hindle, this represents the way forward: 'We have changed our mindset in dealing with campaigning groups over the past few years, and that has definitely benefited us. These are our stakeholders and they have a right to know what we are doing.'[29]

This new culture of openness culminated in the creation of a Global Moms Panel, an advisory group of mothers from around the world. Although it is easy to be cynical about this type of initiative, McDonald's do appear to have been genuine in their attempt to recruit an independent panel of mothers, from different backgrounds, to provide input on a range of issues, such as active lifestyles and children's well-being. McDonald's UK boss Steve Easterbrook is quick to recognise the value of this change of approach: 'I think the one thing that we've changed in the past couple of years is I think we have been a lot more open about engaging in dialogue with people as long as they aim to be constructive, and during that time I think we also continued to make progress in moving our business. I think as we continue to evolve in a progressive way and with a real positive intent, some of those voices have just become a little quieter.'[30] The company has clearly travelled a long way since the days when it felt that the best way to protect its corporate reputation was to take protesters to court.

Twenty years ago, corporations such as McDonald's were worried by activists handing out leaflets outside their stores or writing letters of protest to the media. Now the battleground between activists and corporations has shifted to the Internet, and especially to search engines such as the ubiquitous Google. If you want to see the power of Google as

[29] Quoted in *Marketing Week* (14th February 2008)

[30] Quote from an interview with Jeff Randall, Sky News (14th November 2007)

a mouthpiece for the activist movement, take a tip from online journalist, Jeff Jarvis. He recommends that companies should Google any of their brands, followed by the word 'sucks'. Once you start following Jarvis's advice, it becomes pretty addictive: in fact, it can lead to a new game in the office, in which you compete with your co-workers to identify the company that sucks the most. Inevitably, the usual corporate suspects – those businesses that always seem to be on the receiving end of a consumer backlash – appear to generate the most responses. So typing 'Tesco sucks' generates 152,000 results, 'Wal-Mart sucks' 169,000, 'Exxon sucks' 156,000 and 'BA' or 'British Airways sucks' an incredible 1.6 million results – it must be the owners of all of those lost bags, and this was even before the disastrous opening of Heathrow's Terminal 5. BA's 'suck ranking' was only slightly lower than the figure for George Bush, who remains the number one source of Google-based criticism. What will people do to occupy their Web-surfing time when he finally leaves the White House?

Google is loved by activists because they are able to exploit the complicated algorithm at the heart of its technology, which amongst other things ranks a website according to the number of sites linked to it. By linking its sites, blogs and forums to a specific protest site, the activist community can ensure that its voice of protest appears alongside any official corporate site in Google's 'organic' search process. Type 'Exxon' into Google, and alongside the official www.exxon.com corporate website you will find, pretty high up the search rankings, www.exxposeexxon.com and www.exxonsecrets.org: two activist sites attacking the company's drilling activities and alleged efforts to block action on global warming. The official websites for Dick Cheney's Halliburton are similarly surrounded by a host of activist sites criticising alleged malpractices and cronyism. Once established, these types of anti-corporate protest sites are very difficult to dislodge.

Some businesses have tried to forcibly remove these protest sites with the threat of legal action. However, the experience of US job search company J L Kirk and Associates provides a cautionary tale for any businesses who think they can use their lawyers to hold back the tide of online criticism. The company found itself in a classic David and Goliath dispute with a lady called Katherine Coble. She wrote a lengthy blog, complaining about how the company had treated her and her out-of-work husband.

This wasn't an extended rant punctuated by streams of invective. Katherine told their story in a calm and considered way: 'I am really ticked off at people trying to use fear to motivate others. I don't care if you are a fire-and-brimstone preacher, an insurance salesman, a used car salesman or a cat burglar. Finding someone else's fear and vulnerability and using that vulnerability to somehow enrich yourself is a cheap and underhand tactic. It's wrong and it's cruel . . . My husband and I are not idiots. We both expect to pay for services rendered from any provider. But we generally like to be treated as responsible adults.'[31] These are hardly the words of an anti-corporate agitator.

The magic of the search algorithm kicked in, and Kathleen's blog quickly appeared towards the top of the Google search results for J L Kirk. The company's response? A threatening letter was sent to the Cobles, demanding that they 'take down the blog entry . . . together with the entire thread of comments'. They were also accused of making defamatory statements under Tennessee State law and threatened with 'monetary damages for tortuous interference'. From a legal perspective, J L Kirk's were probably well within their rights to issue such a response. They believed that the reputation of their business was being damaged and that a strongly worded letter from their lawyers would solve the problem. Unfortunately, in this new, hyper-connected world, they simply unleashed a hornets' nest of online protest.

Within hours, the blogging community had picked up the story and, in particular, the way that a company had, in their eyes, attempted to stifle freedom of speech. Kathleen's story was posted on other blogs or linked from other sites, which simply raised its profile in the Google search rankings. Bloggers saw this as a cause célèbre. The comment of one blogger was typical: 'I'm happy to pile on, because this brutish attempt

[31] http://mycropht.blogspot.com

to shut down a person's freedom of expression is an attack on all of us.'[32] Another responded in slightly more colourful terms: 'Don't send bloggers stuff that makes you look like an asshat. They tend to blog about it'.[33]

J L Kirk's attempts to block the complaints made by a single customer simply amplified the impact of those complaints. They also helped to turn Kathleen's story into a legitimate news item, which meant that any blogger could repeat it without fear of legal action. Google the company's name today, a year after Kathleen's story was first posted, and the top ten search results are all blogs writing about the company's dispute with the Cobles. One of them features a YouTube video of the case being discussed on a Tennessee news channel. This was probably not the smartest way to protect a corporate reputation.

Australian software company 2Clix attempted a similar approach, although in this case their target was not a member of the public but a popular broadband forum, Whirlpool. The forum, which features the usual mix of product stories and independent product reviews, had become a focus for critical reviews of 2Clix's accounting software. The company's response was to sue for damages, claiming that the comments made were 'false and malicious'. Yet again, a corporate attempt to stifle opinion backfired. The story was picked up by websites around the world and by the news media in Australia, the US and the UK.

Jo Best, writing for Australian technology website ZDNet, noted how the threat of legal action simply drew attention to the original critical comments made about 2Clix's products: 'Like a computer virus or Chinese whispers, those comments are seemingly self-replicating, making their way into the ears of more tech-heads and more software buyers – presumably what 2Clix had hoped to avoid. If 2Clix had not fired up its lawyers and had not started court proceedings, I would suggest that the user comments that so riled it would have just drifted

---

[32] http://blog.getsatisfaction.com

[33] www.sayuncle.com

into the online horizon after a time.'[34] The legal suit was subsequently withdrawn, and 2Clix is now in administration.

Two real estate agents in Australia have tried a different way to prevent their reputations being damaged by online articles. Rather than sue the writers of critical online comments, they have launched a defamation action against Google itself. Mark Forytarz and Paul Castran, of the Castran Gilbert real estate company in Melbourne, allege that they have been defamed by articles found via Google searches, and that despite being asked to remove links to the offending articles, Google refused to respond. At the time of writing, the case is still going through the Australian Supreme Court, but few commentators believe that they will succeed in their efforts.

Acting like corporate Canutes – trying to hold back the wave of consumer empowerment – didn't help FedEx, McDonald's, J L Kirk or 2Clix protect their corporate reputations. We are sure that, with hindsight, they would all have considered an alternative approach. Their actions may have been correct from a legal standpoint – McDonald's had been libelled in the leaflet distributed by Steel and Morris, Jose Avila's www.fedexfurniture.com obviously represented a copyright or trademark breach, and Katherine Coble may have defamed J L Kirk – but calling out the legal team certainly didn't stem the tide of criticism. It simply turned the complaints of a few individuals into a mass-media news event.

The responsibilities placed upon legal experts to protect corporate reputations and trademarks will inevitably bring them into conflict with the empowered consumer. Bloggers believe that they are protected by the principles of freedom of speech. According to a study by research company YouGov, fewer than half of Internet users in the UK thought that bloggers should be held to the same legal standards as journalists when publishing opinions, and among bloggers themselves, only a quarter believed that they should be subject to the same rules.[35]

---

[34] ZDNet Australia (13th September 2007)

[35] YouGov research on behalf of legal services organisation DLA Piper (13th May 2008)

Similarly, the world's wannabe film directors, who celebrate, parody or spoof the world's leading brands on social-video sites such as YouTube, believe that they have a right of self-expression.

Duncan Calow, a digital media law specialist and partner at DLA Piper, who commissioned the YouGov survey, takes a different view: 'Blogs and online forums may differ from traditional media in their style and purpose, but their content is still publicly consumed and they have the equivalent potential to cause damage and offence, and to infringe others' rights. Far from being immune from the law, user-generated content is in particular danger of falling foul of it.'[36] Despite Calow's advice, most companies are wary of pursuing legal action. As one head of intellectual property admitted to us, with an air of resignation: 'We simply don't have the time to keep track of everything on sites like YouTube and, in any case, if we take legal action against private individuals – kids making videos in their bedrooms – it simply makes our companies look bad. We simply try to focus on the big guys who are making money by infringing our trademarks or the people who are threatening to do real damage to our reputation. Ultimately it is about picking our battles carefully.'

The BBC was forced to make this type of judgement call when the creativity of one of its viewers appeared to threaten the intellectual property of one of its most valuable programmes. An amateur knitter, who uses the name Mazzmatazz (even knitters appear to need stage names), was threatened with legal action by the corporation after she produced knitted versions of various Doctor Who characters. However, this decision was quickly reversed in the face of what *The Times* described as 'a very British outcry'.[37] *Times* readers protested about the BBC's actions and within three days the broadcaster announced that it was planning to support this example of 'fan creativity'. Mazzmatazz has even been invited to meet BBC executives to discuss the creation of a 'limited edition of exclusive promotional products.'

[36] YouGov research on behalf of legal services organisation DLA Piper (13th May 2008)

[37] *The Times* (17th May 2008)

You only have to look at how the recording industry has failed to stop people sharing music and videos to get a sense of the impossible task facing companies trying to protect their intellectual properties. Between 2003 and 2005 the Recording Industry Association of America sued more than 15,000 people for illegally obtaining music content covered by copyright. During the same period, the amount of illegal file-sharing actually doubled. The threat of legal action is clearly insufficient to change consumer behaviour, especially when consumers refuse to accept that they are doing anything wrong.

So how should companies respond to Web-based criticism if threats of legal action won't work? Ultimately it is about managing a debate. Negative comments cannot be blocked, but they can be countered, either with a straight rebuttal or by explaining how the company intends to respond to valid criticism. The fact that all online dialogue can be scrutinised means that companies have to think carefully about how they respond and, more importantly, how their response is perceived. A highly-crafted missive prepared by the legal department that looks fine to senior company managers may be perceived by other people as a typical example of cold, calculating corporate-speak. Microsoft blogger Steve Clayton has some simple, practical advice for any business planning to engage in online dialogue: 'I try and imagine what would happen if the *Sun* (for our overseas readers, a UK tabloid newspaper) were to read it, or my customers, or my competitors, or my boss, or my mum. That usually does it in terms of self-censorship.'

Openness, honesty and reasonableness have to be the watchwords for any corporation entering into a public discussion. It helps if they treat all criticism as potentially constructive, rather than as an outrageous slur on the company's reputation. This doesn't mean that companies should have to deal with abusive comments. Everyone involved in the debate should abide by the McDonald's principles of 'civil dialogue', and companies are well within their rights to refuse to respond to people who fail to abide by these principles.

Companies also need to be robust enough to take criticism and develop a thicker corporate skin. You can never please all of your customers all of the time. In fact, criticism can be a good thing. By closing their ears to negative comments – shutting down the customer complaints department, removing the 'Contact us' button from the website, and calling out the company lawyers – companies are simply cutting themselves off from an invaluable resource of information and advice. Web columnist Jeff Jarvis's typically pithy advice to companies is to 'love the customer who hates you'. It is his contention that the critics are actually doing these companies a favour: 'Now don't get mad at these people. Instead, help them get even with you. For these angry customers are doing you a great favour. They care enough about your product or service to tell you exactly what went wrong. Other customers may just desert you and head to the competition. But these customers are telling you what to fix. Listen to them. Help them. Respond to them. Ask their advice – and they'll give it to you.'[38]

It might pay companies to hire a few more people for their customer complaints departments – especially people who understand how debate needs to be conducted in the online world – and send the legal team on an extended sabbatical, or at least make sure that they are working closely with their marketing colleagues. Crowd surfing does not always mean doing the 'right thing' from a legal perspective, but nor does it mean failing to protect important intellectual properties. It is about picking battles wisely, accepting criticism where it is merited, and ultimately recognising that working with the crowd is invariably more effective than fighting it.

[38] www.buzzmachine.com February 2008

Chapter 3
The Corporate Response

Having set the scene for why many businesses feel themselves to be at the mercy of the crowd, in this part of the book we will analyse the response of some of the world's leading corporations to consumer empowerment. Many of our case studies come from the consumer technology sector: partly because this is an area in which we have strong contacts, but mainly because we believe that the leading technology businesses have been forced to deal with some of the most extreme expressions of consumer empowerment. Foremost among these is the 'open source' movement: the loose network of software developers around the world who argue that software codes should be made publicly available for anyone to change and improve, provided that those changes and improvements are then shared in turn. Perhaps the most well-known example of open-source software is the Linux operating system. This philosophy doesn't go down too well with those corporations that have invested billions in proprietary software products.

The technology companies also face the challenge of dealing with customers, employees, partners and other stakeholders who are right at the head of the adoption curve when it comes to embracing new communications technologies. These people are, almost by definition, avid bloggers and social networkers. Satisfying their demands for Web-based interaction is an almost impossible task.

We start with a review of Dell's journey from blogger pariah to arch-advocate of consumer empowerment. The company's trials and tribulations, and ultimate redemption, provide a powerful case study for any business feeling itself at the mercy of the crowd. Michael Dell is in no doubt about the importance of this new direction for his business: 'What you have now is that the scale and speed of this [blogging] is exponentially greater than before, and that's a great thing for us to embrace and to learn from and to really drive the future of the company on, based on this dialogue with our customers.'

We then compare the very different philosophies of Microsoft and Apple. According to Eric Abrahamson and David H Freedman, the authors of *A Perfect Mess*: 'Because of Apple's status as David to Microsoft's Goliath, it's also tempting to imagine that Apple is the freewheeling, improvising rebel while Microsoft is a lumbering, rigid bureaucracy. In fact, Microsoft has always operated in a usefully messy fashion, while Apple is the picture of rigid order.'[1] We will explore whether Apple's refusal to play to the crowd is something that can be copied by other businesses or is simply a characteristic of its unique business model.

A handful of businesses have become what we describe as crowd leaders, supporting sometimes unpopular causes that take them far beyond their immediate corporate interests. We will examine why businesses such as The Body Shop, Patagonia and Benetton have been prepared to take a stand on sometimes controversial issues, even if this approach risks alienating some of their stakeholders.

Finally, we will address the challenge of the internal crowd. Pharmaceutical giant Pfizer lives or dies by the intellectual and analytical skills of its employees. The costs of developing a new drug are so enormous and the risks of failure so huge that it cannot afford to make things even more difficult for itself by allowing knowledge to be trapped in silos. We will show how, through the use of new technology, the company has been able to encourage the spread of knowledge and information.

---

[1] *A Perfect Mess: The Hidden Benefits of Disorder*, Eric Abrahamson & David H Freedman (Weidenfeld & Nicolson, 2006)

Dell Hell – A Story of Rebellion and Redemption

> *We screwed up, right? . . . These conversations [with customers] are going to occur whether you like it or not, OK? Well, do you want to be part of that or not? My argument is you absolutely do. You can learn from that. You can improve your reaction time. And you can be a better company by listening and being involved in that conversation.*[2]
>
> **Michael Dell**

The image of the blogger has evolved from that of the mad activist – the type of person who in the pre-web days would have written letters of complaint about corporate behaviour in green ink (the colour that customer complaints departments believe invariably signifies a complete lunatic) to the champion of consumer freedom. Bloggers have become heroes. They have the power and influence to shatter corporate reputations and force corporations to change unpopular policies.

Jeff Jarvis does not look like your typical rebel. A slightly scholarly-looking man, Jeff is currently associate professor and director of the interactive journalism programme at the City University of New York's Graduate School of Journalism, and writes a New Media column for *The Guardian* in the UK. Prior to that, he was a journalist and editor of titles including *Entertainment Weekly*, *New York Daily News*, *San Francisco Examiner*, *Chicago Tribune* and *Chicago Today*. But Jeff's primary claim to fame is that he is the lone blogger who sparked a revolt that almost brought the mighty Dell corporation to its knees when it ignored his complaints about a malfunctioning 'lemony' laptop and a terrible customer service experience. His 'Dell Hell' rants posted on his blog, Buzzmachine, attracted links and comments from thousands of similar disaffected Dell owners, and unleashed a wave of criticism of Dell and its products.

[2] *BusinessWeek* (17th October 2007)

In Jeff's words, he had set off a 'raging mob with pitchforks', and they were determined to storm 'Castle Dell'. Many of them came together on the www.ihatedell.net site, and a strange thing happened. After they had finished complaining, a number of them began helping each other, mainly with technical problems but also on how to get the best out of their machines. Dell did nothing. Well, officially, Dell did nothing. Unofficially some Dell employees started responding and chipped in with advice and comments, totally independently of official helplines. When people Googled Dell they discovered, pretty high up the results table, the www.ihatedell.net site. Even today, if you look at the site you can see conversations between employees and people who are about to be interviewed for a job at Dell. Journalists went there and business partners and families of employees and, of course, customers. It became a landing site for anybody disaffected with Dell, and very soon after that, a site for anyone interested in anything to do with Dell – only Dell had nothing to do with it themselves. The whole development became emblematic of Dell's apparent inability to take control of its own corporate reputation.

'Dell Hell' probably reached its nadir for the company when Jarvis unleashed his magnum opus: an open letter to Michael Dell on 17th August 2005. It is as close as you can get to a crowd surfing manifesto, which is why we have chosen to quote it in full. Check out Jarvis's 'free and friendly advice' for corporate bloggers: better still, pin a copy to your noticeboard.

Gentlemen,

Your customer satisfaction is plummeting, your market share is shrinking, and your stock price is deflating.

Let me give you some indication of why, from one consumer's perspective. I won't bore you with all the details of my saga of Dell Hell. The bottom line is that a low-price coupon may have gotten me to buy a Dell, but your product was a lemon and your customer service was appalling.

I shipped back my computer today and only – only – because I wrote an e-mail to you, Mr. George, did I manage to get a refund. I'm typing this on an Apple Powerbook. I also have bought two more Apples for our home.

But you didn't just lose three PC sales and me as a customer.

Today, when you lose a customer, you don't lose just that customer, you risk losing that customer's friends. And thanks to the Internet and blogs and consumer rate-and-review services, your customers have lots and lots of friends all around the world.

I blog. And I shared the story of my Dell travails here. The topic resonated with hundreds more people. Go read the many comments. Too busy? Then have an intern or an MBA do it for you.

And then have them read all the many posts of other bloggers who pointed to my posts and shared their dissatisfaction with your products, service and brand and, in many cases, announced that they were no longer going to buy your name. See some of those posts and you'll learn a lot.

Heard of those new podcast things? Well, you're in one.

Now go read the press this generated, because the press is reading blogs, even if you're not.

Or never mind the press and even the blogs and just go to a food court to listen to what your customers are really saying about you. A VC in Toronto named Rick Segal happened to be in his building's food court when he witnessed this scene:

'I happened to be sitting across from a couple of bank tellers from TD Canada Trust, the bank in our building. These two ladies I'd seen before so I knew where they worked.

'Lady one: I was going to buy a new Dell but did you hear about Jeff Jarvis and the absolute hell he is going through with them?

'Lady two: Yeah, I know the IT guy told me that the cobler blog was recommending we stay away from Dell.'

Okay, after you are done laughing at this, laughing at Scoble's name being mangled, laughing at two random bank tellers talking about some one-line blog entry about some guy pissed off about his Dell experience; after you are done: pay attention.

I'll accept that an IT guy would be reading Scoble's blog. I'll even accept the IT guy offering an opinion which, randomly, I overheard.

The pay attention part: Lots of people (Dell?) are making the assumption that 'average people' or 'the masses' don't really see/read blogs, so: We take a little heat and move on.

Big mistake.

At the same time, as the tech columnist in the Houston Chronicle *reported, you closed down one of your consumer forums, and your own spokesman said that you have a corporate policy of not talking to your customers on blogs.*

Big mistakes.

So allow me to give you some friendly and free advice about these blog things. You can pay for more.

1. Read blogs. Go to Technorati, Icerocket, Google, Bloglines, Pubsub, and search for Dell and read what they're saying about you. Get it out of your head that these are 'bloggers', just strange beasts blathering. These are consumers, your marketplace, your customers – if you're lucky. They are just people. You surely spend a fortune on consumer research, on surveys and focus groups and think tanks to find out what people are thinking. On blogs, they will tell you for free. All you have to do is read them. All you have to do is listen.

2. Talk with your consumers. One of your executives said you have a look-don't-touch policy regarding blogs. How insulting that is: You ignore your consumers? You act as if we're not here? How would you like it if you gave someone thousands of dollars and they ignored you? You're not used to being treated that way. Neither are we. It's just rude. These bloggers care enough to talk about your products and service and brands. The least you can do is engage them and join the conversation. You will learn more than any think tank can ever tell you about what the market thinks of your products. But go to the next step: Ask your consumers what they think you should do. You'll end up with better products and you'll do a better job selling them to more satisfied customers who can even help each other, if you'll let them. It's good business, gentlemen.

3. Blog. If Microsoft and Sun and even GM, fercapitalismsake, can have their smartest blogging, why shouldn't you? Or the better question: Why should you? Because it's a fad? No. Because it will make you

*cool with your kids? No. Blog because it shows that you are open and
unafraid – no, eager – to engage your consumers, eye-to-eye.*

*4. Listen to all your bad press and bad blog PR and consumer
dissatisfaction and falling stock price, and to the failure of your low-price
strategy, and use that blog to admit that you have a problem. Then show
us how you are going to improve quality and let us help. Make better
computers and hire customer service people who serve customers.*

*It sounds so simple, so downright silly, doesn't it? But that's what
you're not doing now. And that's why you lost me as a customer. But if
you join the conversation your customers are having without you, it may
not be too late.*

Sincerely,

Jeff Jarvis

*P.S. I have one Dell left in the house, my son's. And just last night,
he said he had to buy a fan to put under his machine to suck the heat out
so the graphics card won't overheat and slow down every time he plays
a game. He looked online and found that people have complained to
Dell . . . but no one would listen. Do you hear us now?*

Jarvis's wise words were picked up and linked to by blogs, newspapers
and magazines throughout the world. They also hit the spot within
Dell. In July 2006, after months of conspicuous absence from what was
then the biggest hate storm on the net, Dell launched Direct2Dell, its
first venture into blogging and what Jarvis calls the 'conversation'. It
wasn't perfect, and the critics lined up to point out what Dell was doing
wrong in terms of content, tone of voice and the way that the blog was
managed and optimised: the original name for the blog was shared by
a tequila bar in Texas and an XXX-rated site. But at least the firm had
shown itself willing to take part in the debate and create a connection
with its customers, many of them still angry, some just curious, and
others supportive of the company and its products.

Lionel Menchaca, a 17-year Dell veteran, became the main writer
and the editor of this first official Dell blog, and therefore the new
lightning rod for the Dell Hell storm. It is one thing for negative

comments about a company and its products and services to be voiced externally, on channels outside the direct control of the company, but an official forum – allowing critics as well as supporters to comment on a company's performance – means these comments are hosted on the company's servers and under its own brand name. This is when developing a thick corporate skin comes in handy.

Menchaca admits that many in the firm were sceptical at best, although he points out that at least Dell had a heritage of Internet innovation: it was and is their primary route to the customer. When the Dell business first started, this was a major point of differentiation within the marketplace, allowing it to undercut competitors who went through the usual third parties and retailers. However, Dell's Internet experience was based on the old model of online behaviour, where customers came to a company site, interacted and went away. Dell.com and its variants in hundreds of countries around the world were highly effective sales sites, but they were not designed to encourage two-way communication, beyond the standard technical support-style Question and Answer pages.

Menchaca began posting responses to the specific issues raised by individuals within the mob unleashed by Jeff Jarvis. Much of the time this meant referring them back to customer and technical service people, but at least this demonstrated to the crowd that Dell was willing to listen and prepared to act on what was being said. As individuals began to experience proactive calls and what appeared to be real efforts to sort out their problems, they began to talk about it, which meant that, alongside the criticism, positive news stories were starting to come through. Even the instigator of much of Dell Hell, Jeff Jarvis, began to congratulate the firm on getting involved with individual customers and trying to tackle the issues that underpinned many of their complaints.

Menchaca talks candidly about the challenges behind this, and says a huge amount of work behind the scenes had to be done to ensure that when Dell entered the conversation with customers it could act as well as talk. He admits that customers interacting with the firm via the blog gain a heightened sense of their importance and that this means they expect their issues to be dealt with very fast. Delivering a genuine sense of 'immediacy' within the business has sometimes proven to be a challenge.

The first big test arrived just two weeks after Menchaca's official Dell blog was launched. A video of a flaming Dell laptop appeared on the Internet and became a huge viral hit. Here again was proof, it seemed, that Dell products were not only lousy, but dangerous. Imagine what would happen if your laptop exploded into flames on a plane. Through the vehicle of his blog, Menchaca was able to respond, in a newly credible voice. He pointed out that it was in fact a problem with the batteries, rather than the laptop itself, and offered to help customers with the same battery get a replacement. Bob Pearson, Dell's head of Communities and Conversations, points out that this was also the first time that they began linking the blog to negative coverage: 'We linked to all sorts of coverage that was not that flattering to us and we did so regularly throughout this issue. We gained credibility by doing that, and pretty soon people began to realise this was not a Dell problem as such but something a number of manufacturers were going through, only in our case they could see that we were taking it seriously and doing something about it.' The battery problem could have fatally damaged Dell's business. In fact, the firm's professional handling of the situation won it a new reputation for honesty and openness. It was the start of the fight-back.

Out in the blogosphere, and pretty soon after that in mainstream media, things began to change for the better for Dell. Individual complaints did and still do arrive, and customers still get angry at real or imagined product and service issues, but for the most part these are now seen as individual issues rather than the consequence of systemic failure. On the whole, the firm is now seen as responsive and trustworthy. Bob Pearson says that negative comment on the blog has reduced from 48 per cent to 22 per cent, and is still falling.

Dell's final step along the Damascene road to becoming a crowd surfer took place in mid-2007 with the launch of the IdeaStorm Web forum. Within weeks, this open forum for product and service suggestions attracted 5,500 recommendations and 24,000 comments from Dell users. Most importantly, Dell claims that the IdeaStorm community has inspired 21 product initiatives. According to Bob Pearson, IdeaStorm is part of an effort 'to make sure the customer is walking the hallways at Dell. With the average focus group, you go in for an hour or two, give them some sandwiches and leave. With IdeaStorm we may be listening to conversation going on over two months. It's a totally different game.'[3]

Michael Dell is in no doubt about the impact on his business: 'IdeaStorm is creating value. It's creating new products and new services, with the input of our customers. We didn't know what was going to happen, but you know these ideas are out there and why not? Some people said our competitors can see them too, but so what. It's still about your reaction time and anyway, you would rather have that conversation going on here. Some of it was whimsical, some of it was real, some of it was really thought through, some of it was complete nonsense. Not all these things lead to commercial success, but it was amazing to see the energy that was created by unleashing the power of the ideas of our customers and also to see how our people reacted to it.'

Bob Pearson is excited by the ability of IdeaStorm to shape the company's product marketing strategy: 'In February of 2007 we had no plans to launch a Linux PC at all. But we sat in a management meeting and we read the quantity and quality of the input on the subject, and it was pretty clear what people wanted. They suggested it, they voted heavily for it, and so it was down to us to get it to them as quickly as we could.

'That's the thing about IdeaStorm: it's different to a bunch of guys sitting in a meeting room discussing these things, where the winner of the debate decides what the customer wants and what he gets, even if they are wrong or just the most senior person. Now it's there for you to see what people want, in real time.'

Once the decision to build a Linux PC was taken, the crowd was asked what basic Linux platform they wanted, and 'Ubuntu' came back the reply, loud and clear.

[3] Quoted in AgeAge.com (June 2007)

'Another example is Windows XP,' says Pearson. 'After we launched Vista, it became clear that there was still a big demand for XP across our range. In the old days, we would have just migrated to the new system, but now we knew we had customers who wanted the old system and so that is still a choice they have.'

Dell is now working on building out a more public platform for what it calls 'accepted solutions'. When one Dell customer posts an answer to a question posed by another Dell customer – and that answer works and it is validated both by the crowd and the firm – it goes back on to the site and becomes part of a richer customer service solution. Customers solving other customers' problems. What could be more cost-effective for Dell?

The company is also working to improve what it calls the 'back-end' of the system so that there is a seamless flow of suggestions and ideas into the teams responsible for the product or service concerned. Connecting customer problems or needs with the people in the organisation best placed to help them is a challenge for many businesses. In the short term Dell has addressed this issue with a manual system, but senior managers claim an automated solution 'is pretty much agenda item number one for the division leader concerned'.

Dell has also used the thinking behind IdeaStorm to transform the way it engages its own employees and leverages their specialist expertise and knowledge. According to Bob Pearson, the response has been incredible: 'We have seen over 3,000 ideas to date from our own employees, and they range from deeply technical solutions to "we want a better discount" . . . they got a better discount, by the way.' An internal blogging culture has also been encouraged, mirroring developments elsewhere within much of the IT industry. In fact, they have become the primary way in which the company communicates with its employees.

Bob Pearson is excited about the future: 'There are huge new communities coming online these days, over 500,000 new Internet users every day. We have to be focused on them and what they want. And there are big communities that we are only now beginning to address directly and personally, like the 500 million Hindus in India and the 300 million Russian speakers. That's a lot of conversations.'

And Michael Dell himself is now a fully signed-up crowd surfer, sounding almost evangelical when he talks about how 'we sell 40 million computers a year and unfortunately we aren't going to get them all right, and every time that happens it hurts, but you quickly realise that these conversations [about these things] are going to happen, whether that is at CNET.com or wherever, so let's have them happen at Dell.com and let's go do something about it. And let's go get involved in conversations all around the world, and let's shorten our reaction time and improve our ability to learn from this.'

The challenge for any crowd surfer is to keep surfing the wave of consumer empowerment. It is a challenge that Michael Dell believes his company can meet: 'Our relationship with our customers will continue to be more intimate, whether it's co-creation of products and services, or faster and faster response times. It builds on the historical strengths of Dell, which was always about building products to the individual requirements of customers, and I am sure there are a lot of other things that I can't even imagine but that our customers can imagine, and we now have a process that is strong enough to be able to take that feedback and turn it into something. A company this size cannot be about a couple of people coming up with ideas, it has to be about millions of people and harnessing the power of those ideas.' Crowd surfing — Dell style.

Microsoft and the Blue Monster

For too long, Microsoft has allowed other people – the media, the competition and its detractors, especially – to tell their story on its behalf, instead of doing a better job of it itself. We firmly believe that Microsoft must start articulating their story better – what they do, why they do it, and why it matters – if they're to remain happy and prosperous long term. If they can do this, well, we don't expect people in their

> *millions to magically start loving Microsoft overnight, but perhaps it might get people – including the people who work there – to start thinking differently.*
>
> **Hugh MacLeod** (blogging cartoonist and creator of the Blue Monster)

At the last count over 5,000 Microsoft employees blogged. Almost none of them have been message-trained or briefed by the legal team on what they can or cannot say, and yet they talk to millions of Microsoft's customers, competitors, media, partners, legislators, neighbours and other employees, every hour of every day. The PR and marketing departments have almost nothing to do with the output. They prefer to provide only guidance, in the form of what the company calls *Blog Smart Principles*, which are mercifully short.

And this from a company that is beset by people attacking it for a host of reasons, real or imagined, and always under intense media scrutiny and legislator pressure on both sides of the Atlantic. So how have they managed to enfranchise so many employees to talk from the company, and for the company, on so many subjects, without opening themselves up to lawsuits and negative press comment? How can all these Microsoft employees manage to tread the delicate line between the public and the private so successfully, a task that is usually only trusted to grizzled press office professionals with years of experience under their belts who can see media entrapment strategies and leading questions almost before they have been formed in the mind of the interviewer?

The answer, if you ask some of those bloggers, is that the company 'treats us like adults'. According to Microsoft employee Steve Clayton, whose blog Geek in Disguise[4] is one of the best-read in the UK: 'Our guidelines are just that, guidelines. There are more tips on what you should do or can do than on what you can't. But the key thing we are all taught is "Blog Smart". That's the title of the guidelines and that's what

---

[4] http://blogs.msdn.com/stevecla01/

the firm expects. The effect is that we can all talk in our own voices, and as long as we have been smart about what we say, we will be OK.

'Some subjects are obviously out of bounds, and the key thing seems to be that before you publish on your blog, or comment on other people's, remember that this can be read by anyone and interpreted in any way.'

Microsoft's Blog Smart policy is so enlightened it is worth reproducing here in full. Count the times it encourages rather than warns:

Successful Blogging at Microsoft: A Best Practices Guide

Weblogs or blogs have enabled Microsoft employees to connect with customers, build trust, and enable productive two-way dialogue with the industry. The success of Microsoft's bloggers has come from their ability to responsibly use their blogs as a communication tool for the company. The following is a set of simple guidelines to help you be most effective in your blogging and avoid common pitfalls.

#1 – Be Smart

Microsoft employees are trusted broadly to do the right thing. Apply the same common sense to blogging that you would to any interaction or communications with customers, partners and press. Conduct yourself in a manner consistent with the company's values and standards of conduct. Ask yourself the same basic questions before blogging something as you would if you were on stage at a conference, providing a customer briefing, or even speaking to a customer in the seat next to you on an airplane.

#2 – Good Blogging Etiquette

Whether you blog for your family and friends and have an audience of five, or are blogging to help you build better products and customer relationships and are read by thousands, there are some simple things you can do to make the most of your blog:

- Blog often, blog frequently. There is nothing worse than a blog started with good intent that languishes. Don't start a blog unless you are really committed to actively blogging – the world doesn't need any more 'dead' blogs.
- Use a human voice, be yourself.
- Have a thick skin, don't overreact, think before reacting.
- Keep a consistent URL: it makes it easier for people to find your blog. Microsoft employees can host blogs on blogs.msdn.com, the soon-to-be-released blogs.technet.com, or other free services such as MSN Spaces.
- If you are tired, unhappy or stressed, take a break from blogging; don't let it cloud your judgement.
- Respond to comments: blogs work best when they are two-way.
- Write about what you are most passionate about; be your own authority.
- Register your blog on Microsoft.com so that others can find you.
- Link to others, they will return the gesture.
- If you make a mistake, acknowledge and move on.

#3 – Writing a Blog

Blogs are uniquely personal and conversational in tone. Your blog reflects a lot about you as an individual: your personality, your thoughts, your ideas and your passions. The lines between work and personal life can blur together, and blogs are no exception here. Be yourself and share what you feel comfortable with, and be true to both Microsoft and yourself:

- Let others know when you are speaking for yourself. When you are representing a personal point of view, an opinion or commitment, make it clear to your readers that it is such, or use opinion demarcations such as IMO or IMHO.

- Follow the *New York Times* rule: How would this post look if quoted on the front page of the *New York Times*? Or SlashDot?
- Press are bloggers, bloggers are press. Remember that anything you write on your blog can and will be used by journalists and other bloggers. Everything you say is 'on the record'.
- If you are contacted by a member of the press directly, contact your PR representative for assistance. Press may send you mail asking for further information on something you have written about. Rather than getting into an e-mail discussion, politely suggest they contact Microsoft PR.
- When in doubt, ask. Your manager, LCA, your peers and the bloggers alias are all good places to turn to when you have a question involving your blog.

#3 – Confidential Information

You probably deal with confidential information every day. It is important to protect this information when blogging:

- Don't post any confidential code, information, inventions or other material, whether owned by Microsoft or others.
- Don't solicit information that is confidential to others.
- If someone posts a comment on your blog that you suspect they did not have the right to share, delete it.
- Respect your previous employer's confidentiality.
- Don't break news without clearing it through your PR contact.
- Let people know you work for Microsoft. Identify your affiliation with Microsoft in relevant posts or comments so that others have transparency to this fact.
- Talk with your manager and your HR and LCA contacts before selling or conveying rights to your work-related blog postings: under your employment agreement, Microsoft owns the content produced within the scope of your employment at Microsoft.

Blogging is not different from any other communications when it comes to confidential information.

#4 – Feedback

Blogs are a great resource to gather feedback on a product, a plan or an idea. These are some guidelines to make sure that you gather and use feedback the right way to protect both Microsoft and those providing their opinions to you:

- You can solicit, use, and share your readers' opinions about the appearance, usability, quality or desired feature sets or functionalities of Microsoft offerings, or about whether Microsoft should follow a particular course of action.
- Be cautious with how you handle feedback as it could increase our risk of patent infringement if it leads to changes in a Microsoft product or service. Accordingly, if you are involved in product development and want community feedback, educate yourself on patent risks and your team's position on community feedback.
- Do not solicit, review, use or share source code for implementation in Microsoft products or services without LCA approval.
- Do not solicit, review, use or share APIs, file formats, schema or similar items from your readers under any circumstances without LCA approval.
- If your job responsibilities include soliciting specific or detailed community feedback on Microsoft products or services, work with your LCA contact to evaluate the attendant risks and/or to design a streamlined process for handling the feedback.
- Think about if you are best suited to handle feedback on other products: consider asking your readers to submit product feedback to Microsoft websites designed for that purpose (e.g. MSWish and Product Feedback Center).
- Refer any business development proposals to Opportunity Management Center.

#5 - Giving Assistance

Customers look to Microsoft bloggers for help with an existing or future product when they can't find the answer in one of our Web resources. It's great to send a customer away happy with an answer if you can help, but follow these basic guidelines to make sure you are doing the best thing for all involved:

- Give accurate, current and publicly available information when assisting a customer or partner.
- If you're not the expert, don't imply you are or make up the answer. Specifically, security is a really complicated topic where wrong advice can be damaging for the recipient and Microsoft, so unless you are a true expert whose job is focused on security, don't try to go too deep into prescriptive guidance beyond telling people to run antivirus software and use a firewall.
- Don't speak for other product teams.
- Don't forget about other sources of customer support such as Product Support Services, newsgroups, other blogs, user groups and Microsoft and community-run websites. These are good things to put on your blogroll.

As you would imagine given Microsoft's expertise in the development of software, two social media platforms have been created for those employees who wish to blog. These same platforms are also used to communicate with customers, partners and stakeholders.

Microsoft's crowd surfing is not a new departure. The company's employees have participated in Web forums and explored the use of blogs at conferences and meetings for many years. In 2004 they upped the stakes for everyone by launching one of the first online TV shows. It was actually a website that hosted home-made interviews, shot on handy-cams, featuring Microsoft engineers talking about their products and what they were planning. It was aimed four-square at the freelance developer community, who were (and still are) key to Microsoft's success. These are the people who make the add-on products that make the Microsoft operating systems so rich and so, well, useful. The show was called Channel 9 and it was the brainchild of Lenn Pryor, a seven-year Microsoft employee, who wanted to explore the new forms of participative media that were becoming adopted outside the company. His hope was that he and his colleagues could get closer to the huge base of developers (nearly all of whom spend a lot of time online and are, of course, early adopters of this sort of medium) by cutting out the middlemen and going direct. No editor or journalist from an online newsletter or trade publication would judge what they said in this new media. It was them and the developers, one-on-one.

When Channel 9 was launched, it was not at all well received by some people in the firm, and Pryor has talked about receiving 'nasty grams' and being challenged in the corridors. 'Who do you think you are?' and 'Do you know what you are doing?' were the standard comments. Given the wide array of IT cynics out there, ever ready to attack Microsoft, they could perhaps be forgiven for their scepticism. Pryor and his team persisted, and it quickly became evident to the firm that his initiative had started to make a difference, even amongst the most cynical and difficult-to-market-to audiences.

One of Pryor's colleagues and the main voice on Channel 9 was Robert Scoble, who quickly became synonymous with the site and became, arguably, the most famous Microsoft employee after Bill Gates and Steve Balmer. His in-your-face style of interviews and his strident personal opinions, which were often at odds with the company's official view, made compelling viewing. The sight of real Microsoft employees enthusiastically saying it as they thought it was, about the bad as well as the good, attracted hundreds, then thousands and finally millions of viewers. Within six months the site had been visited by 2.5 million people and was linked to thousands of blogs, including those of former Microsoft sceptics. Such links to other blogs are important, as they denote authority and drive visitors to a site.

Each post and new video captured by Pryor and Scoble garnered more and more of a following. Often the real action was in the comments section, with developers, journalists and bloggers joining in the debate on issues that Microsoft, like most firms, had previously simplified in the form of a static brochure, website or one-dimensional press release. Those cynical, hard-bitten programmers, whose daytime hours are taken up with developing applications to work with Microsoft products, just wanted to be heard.

On the most basic level, Microsoft's use of Channel 9 provided the company with an effective way to disseminate news and other corporate information. But very quickly it became evident that it was also a great way to gain valuable feedback from the people whose products made Microsoft's digital ecosystem really work. This commitment to dialogue began to be noticed by stakeholders, shareholders and the media. This was not the behaviour expected of a so-called monopolistic and control-freak company. The Microsoft people appearing on the videos were, well, people. They were enthusiastic, knowledgeable and obviously really committed. Some of them were even pretty funny, and what is more, their willingness to occasionally air Microsoft's dirty linen in public only served to make both them, and Microsoft itself, more likeable.

Steve Clayton, the Geek in Disguise blogger, followed Scoble's lead in pushing the boundaries of employee-driven crowd surfing within Microsoft. He met a UK-based blogger called Hugh MacLeod, famous on the Web for his funny and often dark cartoons. MacLeod was impressed by Steve and his colleagues and was intrigued by the discontinuity between their energy, enthusiasm and openness and his previous impressions of the Microsoft business. After the meeting, MacLeod sent them a cartoon that he dubbed 'the Blue Monster'. MacLeod says: 'It kind of summed up what I felt they were all saying about their firm in different ways.'

MacLeod's cartoon received a favourable response from Clayton and others within Microsoft, and so he posted it on his blog, www.gapingvoid.com, with a brief video from Clayton explaining the background to it. When people in Microsoft saw the cartoon it immediately spoke to them. Instantly it began appearing on the

microsoft.com stormhoek.com gapingvoid.com @hugh macleod 2006

bottom of e-mails, and very soon after that on the back of business cards. Versions started appearing in all sorts of languages as Microsoft employees took it up as an internal rallying cry.

According to MacLeod the headline works on a lot of different levels:

'Microsoft telling its potential customers to change the world or go home. Microsoft telling its employees to change the world or go home. Microsoft employees telling their colleagues to change the world or go home. Everybody else telling Microsoft to change the world or go home. Everyone else telling their colleagues to change the world or go home. And so forth.

'Microsoft has around seventy thousand employees, a huge percentage of them very determined to change the world, and often succeeding. And millions of customers with the same idea. Basically, Microsoft is in the world-changing business. If they ever lose that, they might as well all go home.'

Microsoft, of course, has a brand and a logo and a pretty well-developed sense of what it stands for. It also employs armies of agencies and consultants to think about that brand and the best way to protect and nurture it. Into this highly disciplined brand-building machine

landed Hugh MacLeod's Blue Monster. This more aggressive take on the Microsoft business culture spread like a virus through its 70,000 employees and business partners.

Crowd-driven branding was a new departure, even for a company that was now into its fourth year of empowering internal and external audiences through the use of blogs and social media. But, in the new laissez-faire spirit of Microsoft, the Blue Monster was left to develop in its own way, unconstrained by the corporate branding experts. According to Clayton: 'The Blue Monster totally changed the conversations we were having with our partners ... things would now start off with the debate about how cool the monster was and how much partners enjoyed being part of this movement. Microsoft, at least on the partner side, is not often seen as cool; now we were.'

Even hard-bitten Microsoft haters were engaged. Here's a typical posting from a previously cynical blogger: 'I am now beginning to enjoy Microsoft. Previously I, and I suspect millions of others, perceived MS as a leviathan without a heart. No pulse or warmth. Not a human in sight except Bill in front of a cold global software assembly plant staffed by humanoids. By blogging, you and your colleagues have opened up MS to reveal that the innards are indeed made up of warm people with hearts, with families, with smiles, and wow, you do have senses of humour! This is incredible. Who'd have thought that a corporation like MS was human after all!? We do now. All because you are engaging with us at our level and this is a conversation I relate to and like very much. I hope many more do too.'[5]

The Blue Monster even appeared on a limited edition bottle of wine, which became the tipple of choice at geek dinners and sparked another wave of interest and debate. The *Financial Times* was sufficiently impressed that it wrote a positive story about Microsoft's use of the Blue Monster on the very day that they were also covering the European Commission's decision to uphold their fine on the firm for anti-competitive practices.

Microsoft has won many plaudits for its openness. The company's achievement in creating a management culture that is willing to support people such as Len Pryor, Robert Scoble and Steve Clayton should not be underestimated. Microsoft managers have fought the natural impulse to try to control things. The team behind Channel 9 has been

[5] http://blogs.msdn.com/stevecla01/archive/2007/02/16/another-day-at-microsoft-uk.aspx

given the freedom to talk about the bad things as well as the good. The guidelines for the company's 5,000 bloggers are smart and flexible. The Blue Monster was allowed to do its magic in its own way, without any senior marketing person writing a strategic plan. Microsoft trusts its employees, and it shows.

Why Apple Refuses to Play to the Crowd

> *Your time is limited, so don't waste it living someone else's life. Don't be trapped by dogma – which is living with the results of other people's thinking. Don't let the noise of others' opinions drown out your own inner voice. And most important, have the courage to follow your heart and intuition. They somehow already know what you truly want to become. Everything else is secondary.*
>
> **Steve Jobs**

Steve Jobs is rightly revered as a business leader and a visionary. He's the man who not only co-founded Apple but then came back, after 12 years in the wilderness, to fix the business. His business has a market cap of $105 billion, making it larger than Intel. Even Jack Welch, the doyen of business leaders, has described him as 'the most successful CEO today'. A great salesman and a showman, he is the personification of the Apple brand, but is Jobs a crowd surfer?

Jobs certainly understands and respects the particular crowd that is of greatest importance to the Apple business: the legions of Apple devotees who will queue overnight to be the first in line to buy new Apple products and willingly spread the gospel of Apple to their friends and colleagues. *Wired* magazine has described their behaviour as similar to that of Hells Angels or Trekkies. It has even published a photo montage of people around the world who have the Apple logo tattooed onto their skin. It is difficult to imagine a more overt sign of brand loyalty. With tongue only slightly in cheek, Wired also talked of how 'many Mac fans will make a pilgrimage to Apple's California HQ once in their lives, where they will genuflect before the company sign'.[6]

At the launch of the iPhone in London, *The Times* interviewed one of the hardy Apple fans who had queued overnight in Regent Street to be first in line to purchase the new phone. Graham Gilbert, an owner of eight Apple products, including four iPods and two computers, said he thought it would be fun to 'hang out with like-minded Apple geeks'.

Asked whether his interest in the product bordered on the excessive, Mr Gilbert said: 'It's a bit like a religion. Some people don't understand it and think it's stupid. But then some people also think Christianity's stupid. It's no different really.'[7]

These are the (quite frankly, rather strange) people who kept Apple in business during the tough times; the days before iMac, iPod and iPhone, when Apple was simply a struggling computer manufacturer. They get their annual Apple fix at the Macworld Expo in California. This is the equivalent of Christmas for the Apple devotees, the time when Steve Jobs makes his big new product announcements in front of his army of devoted fans. It feels more like a political rally than a typical trade show. *BusinessWeek*'s Peter Burrows describes Jobs's performance at these events as like 'a rock star, laying down some power chords for Apple's adoring fans.'[8] Jobs's speech is broadcast live by a host of technology websites and the highlights are regurgitated by every technology writer and blogger within hours.

Jobs will do everything he can to retain the loyalty of these Apple fans. When the early iPhone buyers protested after the price of the product was reduced within months of its much-hyped launch, Jobs rushed out a formal apology, admitting that 'even though we are making the right decision to lower the price of iPhone, and even though the technology road is bumpy, we need to do a better job taking care of our early iPhone customers as we aggressively go after new ones with a lower

[6] *Wired* (14th June 2004)

[7] *The Times* (9th November 2007)

[8] *BusinessWeek* (25th September 2006)

price. Our early customers trusted us, and we must live up to that trust with our actions in moments like these.'[9] This personal message was accompanied by the offer of a $100 store credit. It is difficult to imagine any other consumer electronics business doing this. The prevailing opinion appears to be that early buyers should expect to pay a premium for being first in the queue and the bragging rights that follow. They shouldn't therefore be surprised when the price subsequently falls; that is just the way of the market. Jobs clearly doesn't think in this way.

He also recognises the importance of the Apple Stores for the brand devotees: temples to the brand where they can play with the products, see demonstrations, consult experts and hang out with their fellow Apple fanatics. Writing in *The Observer*, John Naughton describes the sense of anticipation that greets a new store opening. It is clear that this is no normal retail experience: 'From further down the arcade could be heard shouting, whistling and general sounds of excited hubbub. Further examination revealed a 100-yard queue of people. Every so often, a steward would motion the 10 people at the head of the queue to enter a store. As they did so, the staff applauded them. Many of the customers took photographs of themselves as they entered. Inside they were greeted by more applauding staff and given a white box containing a complimentary T-shirt, after which they proceeded into the seething emporium. As they left, a smiling staff member thanked them. And from the expressions on the departing faces, it was clear that they had had what in marketing cant is called "a great retail experience".'[10]

Since 2001, Apple has opened around 250 stores, despite the warnings of retail experts that the company didn't understand bricks-and-mortar retailing. They may represent expensive pieces of retail real estate but they are invaluable in turning Apple enthusiasts into advocates. The Apple Stores are also contributing to the company's bottom line. In the quarter to the end of September 2007, Apple reported that its

[9] Open letter to customers, Apple.com (September 2007)

[10] *The Observer* (30th March 2008)

retail stores accounted for $1.25 billion of the company's $6.2 billion revenues, a 42 per cent increase over 2006.

But understanding the crowd and hitting the erogenous zones of the Apple devotees is not the same as truly embracing the crowd. There is a contradiction at the heart of the Apple business that this creator of many of the world's most cutting-edge electronic products continues to adopt a very traditional command-and-control approach when it comes to new product development and stakeholder communication.

Jobs is known throughout Silicon Valley as a control freak. Somebody once described him as a 'dictator with good taste'. Writing in *Fortune* magazine, Peter Elkins is highly critical of Jobs's management style: 'No CEO is more wilful, or more brazen, at making his own rules, in ways both good and bad. And no CEO is more personally identified with – and controlling of – the day-to-day affairs of his business.'[11] Jobs is the only person in Apple allowed to break news, and then only to a small selection of journalists. And the company has certainly not adopted the open-minded attitude to employee blogging that has characterised Microsoft.

Frank Shaw, Waggener Edstrom Worldwide President, heads the Microsoft PR account, so his comments about Apple do need to be treated with a degree of caution. However, he makes some interesting points about the Apple approach: 'It is super-closed – no blogs, no ongoing communication, and most stories/blogs etc. are tied to news events. The image of the company is framed via ads alone and not PR – certainly a safe way of doing things and super, super-controlled.'[12] Jobs is great at whipping the crowd into a frenzy when he launches the latest blockbuster product, but seems less interested in an ongoing, open and sustained dialogue.

Steve Jobs's success at Apple appears to fly in the face of the principles that guide most of the businesses operating within Silicon Valley. The

[11] *The Trouble with Steve Jobs* (*Fortune* magazine)

[12] Frank Shaw's Glasshouse blog

prevailing mantra within the Valley is described by *Wired* journalist Leander Kahney as: 'Embrace open platforms. Trust decisions to the wisdom of crowds. Treat your employees like gods.' Google is seen as the arch-exponent of these New Age principles, encouraging its engineers to devote 20 per cent of their time to pursuing their own interests, an initiative credited with leading to the development of products such as Gmail and Google News. In contrast, according to Kahney, Apple has flouted the Google mantra and behaved 'more like an old-fashioned industrial titan than a different-thinking business of the future'.

The clearest demonstration of the difference between Apple's philosophy and that of other electronics manufacturers is when it comes to new product launches. Steve Jobs and his senior team are the magicians who like to pull rabbits out of the hat; they like to keep new products secret and then unveil them to dramatic effect. Even Apple employees have little idea of what the company is planning. The company is brilliant at preventing leaks: industry experts had a pretty good idea that Apple was planning to launch a mobile phone, but no one outside the company appeared to have any idea of what it would look like. According to Kahney, 'Apple creates must-have products the old-fashioned way, by locking the doors and sweating and bleeding until something emerges perfectly formed . . . In Cupertino [Apple's HQ], innovation doesn't come from coddling employees and collecting whatever froth rises to the surface; it is the product of an intense, hard-fought process, where people's feelings are irrelevant.'

Most of Apple's competitors, especially Dell and Microsoft, take a different approach. They like to tell everyone what they are planning well ahead of a new product launch. Plans will be shared with retail customers, with software developers and especially their business partners. They will have conversations with different people at every stage of the product development process. Key influencers – the most important customers, technology journalists – will be brought onside well before any official product launch. Abrahamson and Freedman, the authors of *A Perfect Mess*, contrast this approach to new product development to the messiness of Microsoft (a good thing as far as they are concerned): 'Apple keeps its developing products under tight wraps until it is ready to introduce them with a big bang as fully-realised gems. Microsoft often throws together, under little secrecy, buggy, ill-functioning first versions of products, and then keeps fixing, shifting and tweaking them until they're the most popular out there.'[13]

This open approach to new product announcements can have its drawbacks, especially when it comes to generating publicity. *Guardian* journalist Charles Arthur, who is clearly a big fan of Steve Jobs's surprises, contrasts the Apple approach to that of Microsoft: 'I can't recall the last time a Bill Gates speech led anyone to hold a middle, let alone a front page.' He also believes that Apple's secretive approach is more enticing for potential buyers: 'pre-release hype ... [i.e. the approach taken by Dell and Microsoft] ... makes people more careful about what they buy. If you tell them that something is coming at some point in the future, they will evaluate everything that's out there very carefully. But if you just drop something into their laps, all they'll think about is the brand. And if they like that, ker-ching!'[14]

Whatever the merits of Apple's approach to new product launches, it is clear that the company does not go out of its way to encourage debate. According to former Apple software developer Jens Alfke: 'Apple's a very focused company, and that's a strategy that's worked well for the past 10 years ... But I'm fascinated with social software and Apple isn't ... I didn't see any place in the company where I could pursue my ideas. It would have meant evangelising reluctant executives into sharing my vision ... And then there are blogs. Apple doesn't like them, not when they talk about it. (Big surprise.) I've heard it said that there are hardly any bloggers working at Apple; there are actually a lot more than you'd think, but they mostly keep it a secret. (I could out a few people, including at least one director ...) I think Apple's policy

---

[13] *A Perfect Mess: The Hidden Benefits of Disorder*, Eric Abrahamson & David H Freedman (Weidenfeld & Nicolson, 2006)

[14] *The Guardian* (21st February 2008)

on blogging is one of the least enlightened of major tech companies; Microsoft in particular is surprisingly open.'[15]

Alfke also makes some interesting points about the command and control culture under Jobs: 'Apple's lack of individuality bugs me. I don't mean internally: within the company, communication is reasonably open and there's lots of room for self-expression. But ever since the return of Steve Jobs, the company has been pretty maniacal about micro-managing its *visible face*, to make it as smooth and featureless as an iPod's backside. It's deeply ironic: for a company that famously celebrates individuality and Thinking Different, Apple has in the past decade kept its image remarkably impersonal. Other than the trinity who go on stage at press events — Steve Jobs, Jonathan Ive, Phil Schiller — how many people can you name who work for Apple? How many *engineers?*'

Compare Steve Jobs's apparent disinterest in the blog as a corporate communications mechanism to that of Sun Microsystems' Jonathan Schwartz: 'Sun is a company with a long history of openness. The importance of open communication among all employees is deeply ingrained in Sun's culture, from the executive team and throughout the organisation. Today we have thousands of Sun employees blogging, including members of senior management ... The topics also range well beyond Sun and technology. Sun employees are interesting people, active members of their communities and interested in addressing global issues. Providing a platform for any of these conversations encourages participation and brings together our heritage of technology innovation and open communications. I can't think of a more appropriate way to interact with the marketplace than by encouraging the entirety of our employee base to do so.'[16]

The blogging community finds Apple irresistible – a survey of UK bloggers showed that it was the most blogged-about brand.[17] The company's reticence when it comes to communication simply

---

[15] http://mooseyard.com/jens

[16] Interviewed in *Industry Week* (1st August 2006)

[17] Prompt Communications' analysis of UK bloggers Dec 07–Jan 08

accentuates the bloggers' interest in Jobs's empire. Although most of the comments are pretty positive, Apple has shown itself to be highly intolerant of the type of Web-based speculation that Silicon Valley tends to take for granted. Self-professed Apple fanatic Nicholas Ciarelli created Think Secret, a website devoted to exposing Apple's new product plans whilst still in his teens. *Wired* magazine's Leander Kahney described Apple's response to this initiative: 'Most companies would pay millions of dollars for that kind of attention – an army of fans so eager to buy your stuff that they can't wait for official announcements to learn about the newest products. But not Apple . . . Ciarelli received dozens of cease-and-desist letters from the object of his affection, charging him with everything from copyright infringement to disclosing trade secrets.'[18]

Steve Jobs and Apple are a contradiction. The crowd, as embodied by their legions of fans, loves the brand; in fact, the success of the Apple Stores shows how they are clamouring to enter Jobs's world. But the business almost seems to go out of its way to avoid dialogue with the crowd, both externally and internally. So does this imply that the refusal to crowd surf need not be an impediment to commercial success? Is the importance of touchy-feely spirit of openness and interoperability that characterises the rest of Silicon Valley overstated?

Technology consultant and author of leading technology blog Andy Lark argues that Apple can only behave in this way because it occupies a unique space in the market: 'Apple's approach works because they are the only player in their hyper-proprietary market . . . The rest of the technology sector is so hyper-competitive and multi-market, other approaches are needed.'[19] Apple is the only vertically integrated business within the consumer electronics market; it creates all of its hardware and software in-house. This means that it doesn't have to collaborate with strategic partners: it can play by its own set of rules, and as long as Jobs and his design guru, Jonathan Ive, continue to wow the market, why

---

[18] *Wired* magazine (18th March 2008)

[19] www.andylark.blogs.com

should they change anything? Some employees will express frustration with what insiders describe as the 'hero-shithead roller-coaster' and complain about the culture of secrecy and the company's attitude to blogging, but people are still queuing up to join the Apple bandwagon. Equally, as long as the Apple fans receive their annual dose of product magic from Jobs and his inner circle and get the chance to experience the brand at first hand in the Apple Stores, they are unlikely to complain that the company doesn't ask them to contribute suggestions for new initiatives.

Steve Jobs is a one-off: a charismatic control-freak, with the apparent Midas touch when it comes to new products. He has built a unique business model and is most definitely on a roll. Even the relatively lukewarm response to the MacBook Air and slow take-up of the iPhone in certain markets has failed to knock him out of his stride. However, Apple is not a replicable model: it is the result of a particular set of circumstances and a very unusual leader. Just because Jobs refuses to embrace consumer empowerment, it doesn't follow that other businesses can afford to follow his lead. In the words of Leander Kahney – in a neat spin on Google's famous catchphrase 'Don't be evil' and with tongue very firmly in cheek – in the case of Apple, 'Sometimes evil works'.

The Crowd Leaders

If you think you're too small to have an impact, try sleeping with a mosquito.

Anita Roddick

They say that the only way to lead a group of Welshmen is to find out which way they are going and then get in front of them. Following this logic, should crowd surfers simply follow the demands or even the prejudices of the crowd? Is it sufficient to be a populist, to simply discover the issues that most matter to employees, customers and shareholders and then act accordingly? This approach certainly has some logic and is undeniably a safe strategy to adopt – who would criticise a business leader for listening to customers or for working in the narrow interests of shareholders?

Most business leaders are populists or crowd-pleasers to some extent; they tend to concentrate on the issues that are most relevant to them and their stakeholders. Oil companies invest their corporate social responsibility budgets on environmental and energy issues; clothing brands have been forced, increasingly, to talk about ethical sourcing and labour conditions; alcohol companies see collaborating on responsible drinking initiatives as a sensible way to keep the legislators at bay. Their primary motivation is to be seen to be doing the right thing in the eyes of the crowd – employees, legislators and especially their shareholders – rather than fulfilling any higher social purpose. Even when they appear to be supporting a cause that will have no discernible impact on the bottom line, there is invariably a degree of self-interest involved. *Financial Times* journalist Andrew Jack provides a typical example from the mining industry: 'While support for causes such as the fight against AIDS might look like good citizenship, for mining businesses such as De Beers and Anglo-American operating in sub-Saharan Africa, where their workforce is heavily affected, it is central to their core needs.'[20]

There is another type of business that chooses to think beyond these core needs, that aims to lead rather than follow the crowd. They have decided to align themselves with issues beyond their immediate corporate interests. Prepared to take a stand on sometimes controversial issues, even if these might alienate some of their stakeholders, they behave more like activist groups than traditional companies.

The Body Shop, under the leadership of the late Anita Roddick, was probably the first major corporation to take a high-profile stand on political issues. Its mission statement opened with the overriding commitment 'to dedicate our business to the pursuit of social and

---

[20] *Financial Times* (5th July 2007)

environmental change'. The company's focus on environmental issues was what you might expect and largely uncontroversial; Roddick was a proponent of recycling and eco-awareness long before these issues became fashionable. Less predictable was The Body Shop's willingness to take on controversial political causes, such as its campaign on behalf of the Ogoni people in Nigeria, whose livelihood and environment was allegedly suffering at the hands of the Shell oil multinational. Filling the windows of the stores with images of human rights abuses is hardly the most obvious way to sell beauty products. The campaign to save Ken Saro-Wiwa and eight fellow Nigerian activists failed – they were executed by the Nigerian government in 1995 – but two years later, Shell issued a revised operating charter, committing the company to human rights and sustainable development.

During Roddick's later years she switched her attention to the battle against the perceived dangers of globalisation and specifically the role of the World Trade Organization. The Body Shop's campaigning ethos was the one thing that differentiated the business in the eyes of consumers, especially once all the other health and beauty retailers on the high street had started selling their own environmental and animal-friendly products. None of Roddick's competitors was prepared or able to take a stand on such political issues.

Speaking at the memorial service for Roddick, on what would have been her 65th birthday, Kate Allen, director of Amnesty International UK, said: 'Anita's lasting gift will be to inspire future generations of activists to stand up, speak out and act together to make the world a better and fairer place.' In an appropriate memorial to Roddick's memory, the date of her birth has been designated 'I am an activist Day' to inspire campaigners in the causes she championed: peace, human rights, climate change, homelessness, trade justice and women's rights.

It is testament to the business acumen of her husband, Gordon, that she had the time to dedicate to so many causes whilst remaining The Body Shop's figurehead. It will be interesting to see whether the business's activist philosophy can survive the double-whammy of Roddick's untimely death and its sale to French cosmetics giant L'Oréal in 2006. When the sale was announced, animal rights activists were quick to threaten a boycott of the stores because of L'Oréal's use of animal testing.

The Lush cosmetics retailer appears to be following the template created by Roddick, launching a campaign calling for the closure of the US detention camp in Guantanamo Bay. As with Roddick's support of the Ogoni, there is no connection between Lush and Guantanamo. It stemmed from a chance meeting between the retailer's co-founder Mark Constantine and human rights lawyer Clive Stafford Smith. Constantine doesn't see a problem with a cosmetics company stepping outside its traditional areas of interest: 'Because Lush is a cosmetics company, we normally campaign over the rights of mice and rabbits being harmed in pointless and cruel safety experiments. But when humans are being treated worse than rats in a cage, we knew it was time to launch an initiative to close Guantanamo.'[21] Anita Roddick would definitely have approved of Constantine's campaign.

Roddick's political leanings are shared by Yvon Chouinard. A world-class mountaineer, keen surfer and all-round action man, he makes Richard Branson look dull and unadventurous. He also found time to create the Patagonia sportswear business, which has blazed a trail for ethical product sourcing and environmental campaigning. Patagonia was the first major retail company to switch all of its cotton clothing to organic, the first to make fleece from recycled soft drink bottles, and the first to pledge a percentage of profits to environmental organisations.

Chouinard is a passionate environmentalist. During the 2004 US Presidential election, he launched his own Vote the Environment campaign in an attempt to get global warming higher up the political agenda. The Patagonia stores provided a focal point for the campaign. He had no concerns that his overt political campaigning would upset Patagonia's customers: 'I'm not in the business to make clothes. I'm not in the business to make more money for myself. This is the reason Patagonia exists – to put into action the recommendations I read about

[21] Quoted in *Brand Republic* (3rd March 2008)

in books to avoid environmental collapse. That's the reason I'm in business – to try to clean up our own act, and try to influence other companies to do the right thing, and try to influence our customers to do the right thing. So we're not going to change. They can go buy from somewhere else if they don't like it.'[22] This willingness to risk alienating some of his potential customers marks out Chouinard as a leader of the crowd; it helps that he doesn't have a bunch of institutional shareholders scrutinising his every move.

Patagonia also plays by a different set of rules when it comes to marketing. Chouinard claims that he can afford the business to grow at what he describes as a natural rate 'which basically means that only when our customers want something do we make more, but we don't prime the pump. We don't advertise on buses in inner cities to get gang kids to wear black down jackets. I basically want to make clothing for people who need it, rather than for people who want it.'[23] No prizes for guessing which businesses he has in mind when referring to what he considers to be the evils of marketing expensive sports brands in the inner cities.

Even the most cynical commentators would hesitate to question the motives of Roddick, Constantine or Chouinard, or accuse them of simply using their support for social or political issues as a clever marketing tool. However, this was the criticism thrown at another company that tried to champion controversial issues during the 1980s and 1990s.

For 18 years Oliviero Toscani was the creative mind behind a series of highly provocative advertising campaigns for Benetton. He always argued that the images he used – a white baby nursing at a black breast; a priest and nun kissing, prisoners on death row, an AIDS patient in the last stages of life, and the bloody uniform of a dead Bosnian soldier – were intended to encourage debate: 'I have found that advertising is the richest and most powerful medium existing today, so I feel responsible to do more than say "Our sweater is pretty".'

---

[22] Taken from an interview by Amanda Griscom Little for her environmental blog, Grist (October 2004)

[23] As above

As far as Toscani and his colleagues at Benetton were concerned, they had a legitimate right to use advertising to make a statement about important social, political and environmental subjects. 'These were photos that portrayed the real world, fell within the conventions of information, and introduced a new and intriguing question about the fate of advertising: can marketing and the enormous power of advertising budgets be used to establish a dialogue with consumers that focuses on something other than a company's products?'[24] These were also the types of issues – challenging authority, attacking prejudice, preaching multi-racial, multi-national brotherhood – likely to appeal to Benetton's younger consumers.

Others accused him of simply trying to shock for the sake of it, and found the juxtaposition of harrowing or controversial issues with brightly coloured knitwear to be inappropriate or opportunistic. The critics argued that Benetton's commitment to the issues highlighted in its advertising was superficial. Walk into one of its stores and you would struggle to find any reference to the causes that Toscani claimed were so important. Unlike The Body Shop stores, which were used to promote Anita Roddick's personal crusades, the Benetton store owners – mostly independent franchisees – were largely unwilling to devote window space or point-of-sale materials to support the advertising messages. Many hated the advertising, claiming that it damaged the happy, sunny image of the Benetton brand. The decision by American department store Sears, Roebuck & Co. to drop Benetton products in the wake of the furore that followed Toscani's use of images of people on death row appeared to confirm their fears.

Toscani resigned not long after the death row controversy, although the company denied that the events were connected. By the time he had left the company, sales were 20 times greater than when he arrived 18 years earlier, so he could argue that, despite the controversy and the complaints of franchise owners, his campaigns had been effective from a commercial perspective.

---

[24] www.bennetongroup.com

Eight years later, Benetton has unveiled a new campaign that once again aligns the business with an important global issue: poverty in Africa. However, the way that it is supporting the Africa Works campaign – a micro-credit programme in Senegal – is markedly different from its approach during the days of Toscani's creative leadership. This time there are no harrowing images; the tone instead is positive, featuring happy Senegalese workers who have used micro-loans to start small, productive businesses. The campaign is also fully supported in-store, with window displays and literature.

Benetton would almost certainly argue that this represents no more than an evolution from the days of Toscani, but it somehow feels more authentic and less superficial. Even the Benetton corporate website talks about how 'the old charge that "Benetton exploits pain to sell sweaters" has been turned on its head. It is the UN and humanitarian groups that are taking advantage of the power and recognisability of the Benetton logo and its sweaters to give voice to the rest of the world.'[25]

Alessandro Benetton, son of founder Luciano and executive deputy chairman of the Benetton Group, accepts that the Africa Works campaign takes his business in a different direction: 'This is the first time for us. It's an experiment. We are investing a substantial amount of money and we believe it is now more challenging to look for enduring action . . . Benetton has never wanted to make a moral statement but it has always wanted to give voice to people or individuals who could not have a voice, and then let the discussion go on.'[26]

Benetton has always seen itself as a crowd leader. The Benetton family is driven by a powerful activist streak and a willingness to take risks. Their campaigning style may have changed since the days of arch-provocateur Oliviero Toscani but, like the late Anita Roddick and Yvon Chouinard, they are prepared to champion issues that take them well beyond immediate self-interest. It is not a direction that every business can follow – there will always be people who argue that the only

[25] www.benettongroup.com

[26] Quoted in *The Independent* (9th March 2008)

contribution corporations should make to society is to maximise profits for shareholders – but at a time when other business leaders bemoan their ability to control the whims and prejudices of the crowd, the crowd leaders are able to set the agenda. They make the waves happen.

Pfizer Looks Inside

> *Teamwork is essential to solving the problems [created by the ageing population]. A chess grandmaster has about 50,000 chunks of knowledge on demand. Our problems are far more complex than that. Therefore, we must work in teams, or circles of trust. The average human has about 150 trusted people within his/her 'grooming circle'. The premise is that circles of trust build slowly and are limited in size. More than half are friends, relatives. A few are business associates. Effective group size is really only about 2–3. Your team is too small to have the knowledge it needs. So, collaboration outside the core group is necessary. The challenge is sharing information intentionally with the best people, at the right time.*
>
> **Rob Spencer**, Senior Research Fellow, Idea Management & Innovation, Pfizer Global Research & Development[27]

To what extent can the principles of crowd surfing be applied to the internal audience? No book on management theory is complete without some reference to the importance of the internal audience. It is accepted almost universally that employee empowerment is a good thing, as is the encouragement of an open culture when it comes to internal communication.

The Dell case study featured earlier in this book has some important messages about the importance of breaking down internal structural impediments if you want to become a crowd surfer. According to the company's eponymous leader, Michael Dell: 'One of the things that a company of Dell's size has to do is to have a set of consistent processes

---

[27] Speaking at the Front End of Innovation conference (May 2006)

to deal with things. It's also important to start small things in an entrepreneurial way, but once you figure out what's important, you can scale it. In this way you can build mechanisms into the system so that these conversations occur, so that the feedback occurs, so that the response occurs and the learning occurs.'

According to Michael Dell: 'We want to involve more teams in this across the company; having product developers, design engineers and people from Dell all over the world involved in this conversation. It's very important for our company as we get even larger, as you always have to bring the outside in. We love customers to tell stories about what they did or did not like so that the teams feel connected, not only in the details of what we need to do, but they feel emotionally connected to the customer.'[28]

The customer service function is on the front line in this new world of the crowd surfer. The people who man the call centres or consumer advice lines are the ultimate consumer champions. This has important implications for the way that they are resourced and managed. It sounds blindingly obvious, but you can't have conversations with people who you don't want to listen to. But this is just what happens when companies fail to put telephone contact numbers or e-mail addresses on their websites because they are worried about the potential volume of incoming calls and emails. Don't they want to know what their customers think? This is what happens when you treat the customer service function as a cost centre, rather than an extension of a company's marketing communications activities. Rewarding call centres, based on the rapid turnover of inbound calls, will also undermine their potential role as a source of customer feedback and knowledge. The irony is that many of the companies that under-invest in their call centre function are quite happy spending hundreds of thousands of pounds on research to try to understand what their customers think.

There is a long and distinguished tradition of companies listening (or pretending to listen) to employees. Employee satisfaction surveys,

---

[28] Interview with Michael Dell on www.buzzmachine.com, 18th October 2007

360-degree appraisals – in which employees are given the opportunity to rate the performance of their line managers – open forums, employee workshops, manager question-and-answer sessions, are all part of the modern internal communications armoury. The Royal Navy ran suggestion schemes as early as 1770, at a time when the line between suggestion and criticism was thin, and being on the wrong side of that line might result in flogging or worse. The first recorded physical suggestion box appeared in Scotland at William Denny and Brothers Shipyard in 1880; whether anyone has bothered to open it in the past 128 years is not known.

According to Mark Turrell, CEO of Imaginatik – a company that provides software consulting solutions in this area – and a keen student of the history of internal communications, the first US company to implement a company-wide suggestion programme was NCR in 1892. 'The concept was based around the idea of the "hundred-headed brain", developed by John Patterson, their infamous CEO. He realised early in his business career that employees had valuable ideas but that management structures tended to prevent those ideas from spreading through the company.

'Employees complained that there was no point giving ideas to their supervisors as the best ideas were stolen, and the worst ideas used as a pretext for their dismissal. Suggestion boxes became popular in the manufacturing sector in WWII and the post-war years. They became part of the total quality movement and an integral part of cost, safety and quality improvement initiatives over the following 50 years. They are still the mainstay of corporate suggestion programmes, be they physical boxes or virtual boxes on company intranet websites.'

Pfizer is the world's largest pharmaceutical company and has been responsible for the development of some of our most important medicines. Medical research and development is an expensive business and involves having a highly specialised employee base. In 2006 they had to relocate some of those valuable staff from Michigan to Connecticut and Rhode Island. The advice they were given going into this exercise was that, despite the generous relocation packages and all the best efforts of the usual HR programmes, only 30 per cent of their key people would uproot their families and make such a move.

According to Rob Spencer, Senior Research Fellow, Idea Management and Innovation, Pfizer Global Research & Development, moving people is no easy task and involves a lot of 'complexity'. Complexity is a favourite expression of Dr Spencer, and he spends much of his time at Pfizer dealing with it.

In this instance the complexity was very human and was 'about my spouse, my kids and my dog', as much as it was about the salary or relocation package. And there is a limit to how far much of this complexity a relocation expert or HR department can handle. The most pressing questions are invariably highly specific and personal and, as a result, they are difficult to deal with. Spencer gives some concrete examples: 'We had people who had kids who were at a particular grade at piano and wanted to know they could get access to the right sort of teachers. Another person had a child who was autistic and so wanted to know if there was a special school within 30 miles of Norwich, Connecticut. Others might ask about synagogues near New London, Connecticut.'

The people best placed to respond to these types of question were the Pfizer employees already working at the facilities in Connecticut and Rhode Island. The challenge was creating a system that would allow the employees in the different locations to interact with each other. Spencer used a software solution from Imaginatik that would allow questions from the Michigan employees to be posted and then answered on a private website. Answers trickled in at first but, as news of the first useful successes spread at the Michigan location, more questions were asked. Human nature at its most helpful meant that the responses to these questions from employees based in Connecticut and Rhode Island became more numerous, quicker and richer. According to Spencer: 'We had instances where an individual would respond that they did not have the answer to a particular question but would provide the phone number of a neighbour or a friend who they thought could help.'

Hundreds of questions were posted by the Michigan employees and most were answered. The system also showed that ten times as many people read the questions and answers as actively participated, which, if nothing else, demonstrated to the Michigan employees that their colleagues in Connecticut and Rhode Island cared about them. When it came to the move itself, 70 per cent of Pfizer's most valued employees agreed to move from Michigan to the other sites, more than double what had been anticipated. Highly trained and expensive resources in a company that, more than most, survives on brain power were retained because the company was smart enough to provide a system and an environment in which one crowd felt comfortable to talk to another.

The company was so impressed by the software that it started to apply it on an ongoing basis, rather than simply use it to facilitate employee dialogue during periods of major change such as a relocation programme. Pfizer describes the process as Idea Management, and makes the analogy with eBay which Spencer characterises as 'a way to connect someone who has an old chair with someone willing to pay for it.

'Idea Management is a way to connect people with a problem with people who have pieces of the solution. Three things are needed to make it work: framing good questions from empowered sponsors, generating and managing ideas at scale, and finally, finding or creating an architecture that supports these properties.'

So far the primary focus for Idea Management within Pfizer has been in the area of research and development, the engine room of the firm's ability to bring new drugs and treatments to the market and to make money. The company has a population of 11,000 R&D specialists in locations around the world working on hundreds of projects. They are highly trained scientists – many with PhDs – and are at the leading edge of science in a host of specialist subject areas. Spencer explains the particular challenges the company faces: 'In this environment, our expectation of getting a valuable answer to the questions that disease and patient needs pose can be very low. We operate in the area of technical long-shots because what we do in R&D is at the incredibly complicated intersection of physical chemistry, synthetic chemistry, the metabolism of the body, side effects and of course, economics. In R&D we set serious product questions, and it is very rare we have them answered because if it does not work, you cannot just make it up or wish it so.

'And the cost of getting a new drug to market is up to a billion dollars. Our attrition rate for ideas that have reached an early stage of acceptance and for which we have already sunk a couple of million dollars is between 20 and 100 to one. This sort of economics and complexity forces you to focus early and get really deep. And in an organisation like a big company, that means we have very specialised teams looking at individual aspects of totally different disease areas in all parts of the world. There are bound to be silos. And yet, despite our fundamental need to focus, sometimes there can be great secondary values to be found in the research we are doing.'

In other words, data or ideas generated by one team working on, say, an asthma drug may have an application for another team working on drugs to treat a completely different medical condition. Many companies find it hard to share this type of knowledge; employees either adopt the philosophy of 'knowledge is power' and wilfully refuse to share what they know, or the internal communications mechanisms do not facilitate the easy transfer of knowledge and ideas. The difference for a company such as Pfizer is that finding ways to break down knowledge silos can mean major breakthroughs and significant health and economic benefits. Spencer is a believer in Linus Pauling's adage that 'the best way to have a good idea is to have lots of ideas'. He describes the standard response in the firm when they manage eventually to match up a question with a solution: 'One side will say "This is fantastic, why didn't you tell me this before?" And the other side will say "Why didn't you ask me before?" ' Of course they're both right – the dilemma is not so much that people don't know the answers, as that they don't know the precise question when it matters. His job therefore is to make that collision happen as often as possible, and he does this through something called Idea Farm.

Idea Farm, which Spencer describes as a diverge/converge process, starts with an e-mail which he sends to his research population, containing a very specific problem posed right up front. 'As specifically as I can, I describe a product that is at a pretty late stage of development. I provide all its details and as much as I can about its anticipated use or primary indication and the financial opportunity it affords us.' And he expects a very low response in return.

'If I send that mail to four or five thousand researchers, I am lucky to get a five per cent return, and it can be as low as one per cent. But that's OK, because what we do and what I have asked is so specific that only a few will have a contribution to make. But the cost impact of one of these ideas moving our project on is huge, and so that return is more than acceptable.'

Pfizer is understandably cagey about elaborating on the particular breakthroughs that have resulted from this crowd surfing approach to R&D – the pharmaceutical industry is highly secretive. However, Spencer claims that in one instance the company was able, through this technique, to identify a molecule in one group that had promise for a piece of work that was being undertaken in another and were able to go almost immediately to what the industry calls a Phase 3 trial, thereby saving themselves years of work and a huge amount of R&D investment. Given the numbers involved, it is no surprise that the company sees the need for a technology infrastructure to manage this. Pfizer has even taken a minority stake in the company, Imaginatik, which provides this platform.

Wal-Mart, the world's largest retailer, is another business that has looked to technology to harness the power of the internal crowd. In recent years, Wal-Mart, in common with all major retailers, has spent a great deal of time looking at its environmental impact and ways in which this can be minimised. It goes out of its way to help customers make informed choices about products, but when it came to stamping out waste or inefficiency internally, they too used a software interface that made it easy and even popular for their employees to make suggestions.

One idea that came from Wal-Mart's software solution was to remove the light in the back of vending machines in the staff canteens, on the basis that staff did not need to be sold to and could see clearly enough the drink options on display. Across the firm's retail estate, this idea alone netted a three million dollar saving. Suggestions such as this rely on the familiarity of the internal crowd with the everyday detail and minutiae of a business. When a firm is looking for operational efficiencies that can be replicated at scale across an enterprise, the ideas can only really come from its own employees.

Among the most sophisticated ways to elicit employee feedback are 'prediction markets'. These reflect James Surowiecki's theories about the wisdom of crowds, by involving employees in predicting how customers or a market will behave. Companies such as the retailer Best Buy in the US use prediction markets to help them forecast customer demand for new products or irregular purchases, such as fridges. The opinions of the people on the shop floor – who spend their time talking to customers and selling the merchandise – have as much value as, if not more than, those in the head office buying departments. Prediction markets are a way of unlocking this expertise. The secret of prediction markets is anonymity: employees make their predictions on the basis of what they think will happen, rather than what they think the boss wants to hear.

The type of technological solutions pioneered by Pfizer, Wal-Mart and Best Buy represent the first serious attempts by major corporations to harness the expertise of the internal crowd. Not only do they generate ideas and solutions, but they have also been proven to increase employee loyalty and productivity. The crowd is flattered to be asked for its opinion and is only too willing to collaborate. Companies have always claimed their people – or 'talent' to use the current HR vernacular – are their most important resource and the basis for their competitive advantage. Concepts such as Pfizer's Idea Management will help turn this management cliché into a reality.

Chapter 4
A Political Perspective

> *There is a connection waiting to be made between the decline in democratic participation and the explosion in new ways of communicating. We need not accept the paradox that gives us more ways than ever to speak, and leaves the public with a wider feeling than ever before that their voices are not being heard. The new technologies can strengthen our democracy by giving us greater opportunities than ever before for better transparency and a more responsive relationship between government and electors.*
>
> **Robin Cook MP**

Business leaders can learn much by studying the behaviour of politicians. In most of the developed world, the leading political parties are faced by declining voter turnout and widespread political apathy. This situation is being challenged by a new generation of politicians – forty-somethings like Barack Obama and David Cameron, and the slightly older Nicolas Sarkozy – who believe that new technology can play a critical role in re-igniting the enthusiasm of the electorate. For this generation, the number of friends you can acquire on Facebook is almost as important as the opinion polls.

We will describe the emergence of this new form of interactive or two-way politics that is, ironically, almost a throwback to the 19th-century style of robust political debate. It is not simply that a younger generation of politicians has embraced social networking, blogging and a host of other technologies. They have also changed the way that they interact with their electorate. As we will demonstrate, it is not something for the faint-hearted politician who feels the need to hide behind the carefully stage-managed political machine, or who cannot deal with robust criticism from real members of the public.

In June 2008, Barack Obama secured the Democratic nomination for the US presidential campaign. Obama's success, especially in engaging younger voters, reflects his willingness to adopt what we would describe as a crowd surfing approach. His use of social networks and some of the new media technologies exploited by his supporters represent the way forward for all politicians, and could be applied equally to the business world.

Politicians Rediscover the Power of Debate

> *Today, reason is under assault by forces using sophisticated techniques such as propaganda, psychology and electronic mass media. Yet, democracy's advocates are beginning to use their own sophisticated techniques: the Internet, online organising, blogs and wikis. Although the challenges we face are great, I am more confident than ever before that democracy will prevail and that the American people are rising to the challenge of reinvigorating self-government.[1]*

Al Gore

The US Presidential campaign of 2008 has been dubbed by many commentators as the first true Internet election. Candidates are falling over themselves to appear ever more Web-savvy, unleashing a flurry

---

[1] Quoted on www.amazon.com

of blogs, YouTube videos and online debates. For the first time, the Web became a mainstream weapon for political campaigners, a way of igniting the enthusiasm of political activists and re-engaging a previously apathetic electorate.

According to Tom Baldwin of *The Times* newspaper, writing about the 2008 campaign: 'Collaborative blogs such as the anti-war Daily Kos now have readerships rivalling those of national newspapers, and increasingly behave – and indeed are courted – as if they are part of the political establishment they ostensibly decry. At the same time, social networking forums such as MySpace and Facebook provide campaigns with access to mounds of fresh ammunition, untapped legions of donors, and armies of previously unmobilised activists.'[2]

British political commentators, observing the US campaign, have already begun to talk up the role of the Internet in the next British election. Tim Montgomerie, editor of conservative-home.com, describes how: 'The next campaign is likely to be remembered as Britain's first Internet election. It will certainly be the first election when bloggers have broken a large proportion of stories. It could be the first election when the best political ads are made on the home computers of political geeks rather than the glassy offices of expensive advertising agencies.'[3]

New media also played a key role in engaging the interest of the electorate during the 2007 French presidential campaign. Loic Le Meur was recruited by the Sarkozy campaign team after they saw the popularity of his independent campaign blog. He was responsible for managing Sarkozy's online debates, and set himself up as the conduit between the Sarkozy camp and the French blogging community: 'We started having a very close relationship with bloggers from all political areas of society, invited them to the campaign headquarters every week to meet a political figure. About a thousand bloggers showed support to Sarkozy, many others who would not vote for

[2] *Fear and Blogging on the Campaign Trail* (*The Times*, 29th December 2007)
[3] Writing in *The Spectator* (9th June 2007)

him were still happy to be in touch with us and with the dialogue that was created.'[4]

Le Meur was able to persuade the previously reluctant Sarkozy to embrace a wide range of Web-based campaigning tools. Sarkozy supporter groups were set up on the leading social networking sites. He even created an island, 'L'Ile Sarkozy', within the Second Life virtual world. Le Muir describes the unusual challenges presented by this particular initiative: 'We survived attacks from opponents which were interesting to see: bombs, naked people, insults, mines dropped, weapons, demonstrations . . . The island has been packed during the entire campaign . . . The most interesting for me was when we started streaming the debates at the real headquarters in the virtual headquarter on SL and had lots of interactivity. We took questions from SL and had the political figure answer them. The conversation and bridge between the virtual and the real life was fascinating.'

The person often credited with pioneering the use of the Internet as a political force is Joe Trippi, the man behind Howard Dean's 2004 US presidential campaign. Dean's campaign failed to last the course, but Trippi's use of the Internet to galvanise grass-roots voters briefly transformed Dean from a long shot into a front-runner. Within a year, Trippi and his team had raised more than 50 million dollars for their candidate, more money than had ever been raised for a Democrat candidate and mostly through donations of 100 dollars or less. In his book *The Revolution Will Not Be Televised*, Trippi talks about enlisting the support of 'an army of almost 600,000 fired-up supporters, not just a bunch of chicken-dinner donors but activists, believers, people who have never been politically involved before and who are now living and breathing the campaign. Through them, we have tapped into a whole new vein of democracy and proven the Internet as a vibrant political tool.'

Despite the failure of the Dean campaign, Trippi remains bullish about what he and his team had achieved. 'An amazing thing happened in the presidential contest of 2004: a candidate lost but his campaign

---

[4] www.loicmeur.com

won. This was nothing less than the first shot in America's second Revolution, nothing less than the people taking the first step to reclaiming a system that had long ago forgotten they existed. This was democracy bubbling to the surface, flooding the landscape and raising all of us – an obscure Northeastern governor, his inexperienced supporters and a handful of old political warhorses – along with it.'[5]

Some of the more idealistic commentators have gone as far as suggesting that, by embracing the Web, campaigners such as Joe Trippi have helped revive the democratic process itself. They argue that the Web, by holding politicians to account and providing a voice for the electorate, becomes a means of challenging voter apathy and re-engaging people in the political process. It also allows politicians to speak directly to voters rather than through the sometimes unreliable filter of the mass media. According to Trippi, recalling the Dean campaign, Internet bulletin boards, websites, chat rooms and Web logs were 'the one place where the ubiquitous presence of television couldn't distort his message'.[6] *BusinessWeek*'s Richard Dunham is equally bullish: 'The Information Revolution is likely to democratise politics by weakening the elite's grip on information.'[7]

The Internet can also allow the electorate to punish these elites. The downfall of US politician George Allen is typically held up as an example of how the Internet can help the electorate destroy as well as build political reputations. Allen's use of a racist term to describe one of his opponent's party workers during the 2006 Congressional elections appeared on YouTube, went viral and allegedly cost him the election.

At the launch of his user-generated television channel, Current TV, in the UK, Al Gore reiterated his belief in the power of new media

---

[5] *The Revolution Will Not Be Televised: Democracy, the Internet, and the Overthrow of Everything*, Joe Trippi (Regan Books, 2004)

[6] As above

[7] Included in *'Quotations on the impact of the Internet on politics and political activism'* (www. hillwatch.com)

to revive the democratic process: 'Democracy, or government by the people, depends on the people being well informed . . . Viewer-created content [the bedrock of Current TV's output] puts power back in the hands of the people, allowing them to re-engage with the issues of the day, as their voices are heard and stories relevant to them are told . . . What we need in TV, as on the Internet, is a multiway conversation that includes individuals and operates as a meritocracy of ideas.'[8]

Other commentators are more cynical about new media's ability to revive democracy. The former editor of *The Observer* website, Rafael Behr, believes that the way social networks operate, and especially the way that Web-based communities can react with extreme hostility to the proponents of rival opinions, makes them fundamentally unsuited to politics: 'Anyone who has spent time blogging will have noticed how people on the Web coalesce into homogeneous groups, based on age, class, tastes. Tribes form and reinforce their identity with codes and shibboleths. Opinions are expressed and arguments made. But minds are rarely changed. This is a problem for politicians who need to build loose coalitions of supporters from different backgrounds and different generations.

'Democracy needs to be more than a collection of discrete peer-to-peer conversations. It requires the accommodation of mutually exclusive views under a covenant of tolerance. It requires that citizens accept membership of a single community and moderate their behaviour towards one another, even when they disagree.

'The Web is no community. It is brilliant for some things. It does information, misinformation, entertainment and commerce. It does freedom. But one thing it doesn't do is democracy.'[9]

Realising Al Gore's vision of the Internet and new forms of user-generated television content as a way of reviving the democratic process will also require a change of behaviour by politicians and their campaign teams. The Internet can provide a perfect platform for political debate,

[8] Quoted in the *Guardian* (12th March 2007)

[9] *The Observer* (17th February 2008)

but too few politicians appear to have embraced the opportunity. Stephen Coleman of the Oxford Internet Institute, an academic centre focused on studying the societal implications of the Internet, describes how: 'Politicians used to put out leaflets with pictures of their family and pet dog and copies of their lousy speeches, and it would be enough. Unfortunately many politicians now just create a website with pictures of their family and pet dog and their lousy speeches, but it is not good enough.'[10]

Andrew Rasiej, who tracked the use of the Internet in the 2008 presidential campaign on his website, TechPresident, has argued that most politicians treat the Internet as 'direct mail for the 21st century, an exercise in top-down control where they create the message, and tell us how to vote and where to send the money.'[11] This is an important distinction that could be applied equally to the commercial world. Despite all the talk about engaging customers or other stakeholders, the majority of politicians, like the majority of business leaders, still think in terms of one-way communication: it is about getting out the message, rather than taking part in a debate.

This is a theme echoed by Tim Montgomerie, who argues that 'the creative side of the Internet isn't properly understood by Britain's political parties. They still see the Web as a way of providing superior distribution channels for unchanged messages. They are in Send mode – analogue politicians in a digital age.'[12] This soundbite had been used previously by Montgomerie's political master, Conservative leader David Cameron, in a House of Commons speech attacking political rival and (at the time) soon to be prime minister Gordon Brown: 'The Chancellor sees himself as a rock upon which Labour can rebuild their church. Instead he is the roadblock stopping Britain meeting the challenges of the future. He is an analogue politician in a digital age. He is the past.'[13]

---

[10] Quoted in *Campaigning in cyberspace*, Becky Hogge (www.opendemocracy.net)

[11] Quoted in *Fear and Blogging on the Campaign Trail* (*The Times*, 29th December 2007)

[12] Writing in *The Spectator* (9th June 2007)

[13] David Cameron's response to Gordon Brown's Budget Statement (22nd March 2006)

David Cameron, as befitting someone of his generation, clearly fancies himself as a digital politician. He is a devotee of Google's annual Zeitgeist conferences, in which the world's commercial, technological and political leaders worship at the shrine of the mighty search engine. Having paid for Cameron's flight to the 2007 Zeitgeist gathering in California, the Google-ites will have been suitably gratified to hear the Conservative leader describe Google as 'responsible for a large portion of the wonders of our modern world'.[14]

In addition to extolling the virtues of Google, Cameron has embarked on his own experiment in political crowd surfing, creating www.webcameron.org.uk as part of his declared ambition to make the Conservatives one of the most technologically progressive parties in Europe. The webcameron site hosts written and video content posted by the Cameron team, plus guest bloggers such as US presidential candidate John McCain. Once registered, readers can post comments, contribute to the forum, add new topics for discussion and pose questions to the Tory leader – many of which Cameron responds to.

The site's first video blog featured Cameron washing up in his kitchen while his family ate breakfast, describing his objectives in creating webcameron: 'I want to tell you what the Conservative party is doing, what we're up to, give you behind-the-scenes access so you can actually see what policies we're developing, the things that we are doing, and have that direct link . . . watch out BBC, ITV, Channel 4, we're the new competition. We're a bit shaky and wobbly, but this is one of the ways we want to communicate with people properly about what the Conservative party stands for.' Cynical commentators questioned why he hadn't bothered to invest in a dishwasher, but the response of most Conservative party supporters to this initiative appears to have been positive.

According to former Google employee Sam Roake, who was responsible for webcameron alongside Cameron's closest adviser Steve Hilton: 'Opening up like this involves a certain amount of risk,

---

[14] David Cameron: Speech to Google Zeitgeist Conference, 12th October 2007 (www.conservatives.com)

but we're confident that on balance it's going to be a great thing – it heralds significant change in the way politics has been done. It very much represents the values of David Cameron's Conservative party, of openness and community. We see this site as being a way that people can engage with politics in a meaningful way on their own terms, and share a platform with David Cameron and thought leaders around the world on the guest blog, which we think is going to be very powerful.'[15]

The most recent initiative from the Cameron camp has been the creation of a social networking site to recruit supporters. For free, or for as much as you would like to donate, you can become a 'friend' of the party – not a full-time member with all the commitment that involves, but someone with a more loose and transitory relationship more akin to that of a Facebook friend. Indeed, the recruitment for Conservative 'friends' has been via social networking sites like Facebook, MySpace, iVillage or Bebo. For many this represented a cheapening of the political process, but what it really showed was that Cameron's Conservatives were totally in tune with a new type of voter, who might have an interest in politics but was unlikely to stuff leaflets through doors or attend dull meetings in church halls.

Politics in the UK and in many other places has been as much about tribal, family or class loyalties as it has about the competencies of individual parties or the appropriateness of their policies, so the idea that you could sign up, for free and maybe only 'for now', and could as easily move on is indeed new. It is not a replacement for party politics, but as a parallel method of involving and engaging a new younger audience – traditionally less interested in party politics – it is a bold new experiment and deserves to be watched closely.

If nothing else, it helps to reinforce Cameron's image as a New Age, digital politician, especially when compared with PM Gordon Brown, who, despite all of the efforts of his advisers to make him more Facebook-friendly, continues to struggle to shake off his 'analogue

---

[15] Quoted in *The Guardian* (30th September 2006)

politician' moniker. It didn't help that one of Brown's last acts as Chancellor was to scrap the Home Computing Initiative that allowed companies to loan PCs to their staff as a tax-free benefit.

Labour's disastrous performance in the 2008 local council elections and loss of the London mayoralty is being blamed partly on Brown's inability to connect with the crowd. He may be more intellectually rigorous than his predecessor, but even his most loyal supporters accept that he lacks Blair's communication skills and populist touch. A natural introvert, he looks uncomfortable in front of an audience, whether at Prime Minister's Question Time, at a campaign rally or on YouTube. Writing in the *New York Times*, Sarah Lyall described how Brown 'loathes the cut-and-thrust of parliamentary debate, particularly when things get rough and the opposition starts making sarcastic comments meant to wound and draw laughs. While Mr. Blair could affect breezy insouciance under attack, Mr. Brown just gets petulant, irascible and defensive.'[16]

It is also difficult to imagine Brown coping with the confrontational and often irrational behaviour of the Web-based electorate. He will no doubt concur with the views of many 'analogue' politicians that the Internet remains a frightening and anarchic place, an asylum in which the lunatics may not be in charge, but certainly have equal access to the building.

Conspiracy theorists, fundamentalists of all political persuasions, tricksters and the just plain weird wait to trip up the unsuspecting political candidate. It is no place for the thin-skinned or those unprepared or unwilling to be mocked and vilified, hence Brown's predicament. In this sense, it is similar to the 19th-century political hustings, in which candidates risked verbal abuse and occasional violence in the name of democracy. Historian Dr J M Lawrence describes the mood of the time: 'Throughout the 19th century there was a strong sense that the public had a right to interrogate its would-be rulers – hence the widespread custom of heckling at meetings and

[16] *New York Times* (5th December 2007)

the surprising degree of tolerance shown towards more disorderly expressions of popular feeling such as the disruption of meetings and free fights in prominent public spaces. Two factors lay behind this rather liberal approach to political order. Firstly, many saw elections as a useful test of a politician's character – if a man was able to govern the nation he should also be able to govern a meeting of his supposed inferiors, and govern himself when faced by the challenge of an unruly mob. Secondly there remained a strong sense, derived in part from classical thinking, that a healthy polity was based upon a vigilant and assertive citizenry.'[17]

Modern political leaders would be well advised to take an equally positive view of the merits of today's 'vigilant and assertive citizenry'. It may come as a shock, after decades of careful stage-management and party control, but as in 19th-century Britain, the smartest political minds should welcome the opportunity to debate their policies with real people, rather than simply preach to the converted. It is, after all, an approach that is still credited with contributing to John Major's surprise 1992 UK election win.

During the 1992 campaign, Major decided that the formal campaign meetings, in which he fielded questions from an invited audience, were too orchestrated and that they were not allowing him to get close enough to 'real voters'. To the derision of many in the media, he reverted to one of the oldest forms of political debate: he stood on a soapbox in the middle of a crowd of real voters and despite much barracking, traded arguments with the crowd with a hand-held microphone. Although this stunt did little to get his policies across to the electorate, it had the effect of reinforcing voters' image of Major as a down-to-earth politician. Had the Internet been a factor in the 1992 campaign, you can be sure that Major would have embraced the opportunity to take his soapbox online.

When politicians put themselves at the mercy of the crowd – whether in public meeting places or online – the way that they respond to criticism is an important test of character. Even Tony Blair, the

---

[17] *Electing John Bull: The Changing Face of British Elections 1895–1935* (ADHS, 2005)

consummate performer at Prime Minister's Question Time and on the conference platform, was vulnerable when confronted by ordinary members of the public and forced to defend government policy off-the-cuff. The only time he appeared vulnerable during the 2001 election campaign was when approached in the street (and in the full glare of the media) by a lady called Sharon Storer, whose partner was being treated for cancer in a local hospital. Blair's somewhat flustered and embarrassed response to her criticisms about standards of hospital care made him look evasive and out of touch. Storer's public criticisms were far more potent than the attacks mounted by his Conservative opponents.

Nicolas Sarkozy has also failed the crowd test. Still reeling from the criticism that followed his rapid and very public wooing of Italian model Carla Bruni, he was captured on video shouting insults at a man he had argued with at a trade fair. This was posted by *Le Parisien* newspaper on its Internet site, attracting more than half a million views within a matter of hours and generating a barrage of criticism from the media and his political opponents. Apparently minor incidents such as this have a nasty habit of undermining political reputations.

Someone once said 'all politics is local', and arguably this is where crowd surfing will have its greatest political impact. One of the transforming qualities of the Internet is the ability of anyone with a broadband connection to have access to a huge and increasing amount of the world's communal knowledge. This, allied to the ability to conduct ever more accurate online searches, is transforming the way in which local pressure can be applied to local issues.

In the UK, the BBC is trialling something called Action Network[18]. It is a technology-based solution that puts people dealing with local issues – planning disputes, environmental problems, hospital closures – in touch with other people in different parts of the country facing similar issues. On its website it claims: 'Action Network can help you change something

---

[18] www.bbc.co.uk/dna/actionnetwork/A2109764

in your local area. Get in touch with people who feel the same way and get advice on taking action.' So if you had a motorway that was being driven through a local piece of greenbelt and wanted to know how to protest and resist, the network would put you in touch with people who had been in the same position and had mounted similar campaigns.

The power of technology-based solutions such as Action Network is simple to imagine. The accumulated knowledge of activism and political campaigning becomes available to all and is no longer the preserve of highly paid political campaigners, public affairs gurus, lobbying specialists or NGOs (non-governmental organisations). Campaigning techniques, and indeed the laws and processes that they seek to affect, can now be addressed by local people.

Action Network has helpful sections on: What can an MP do for you? What can a councillor do for you? What can an MEP do for you? It lists all the major types of local issues from planning to the environment and then suggests techniques for addressing them, and provides links to NGOs or national campaigns that are interested in the issue too. One example is affordable rural housing, an increasingly contentious issue in the UK, where property prices have been rising for years and in some areas rising faster because of the fashion for second homes, making housing unaffordable for local people. Action Network provides a host of tips on how to address this issue, even down to where to go for grants and help to build and develop affordable homes.

The availability of search engines and blog search engines, such as Technorati, now means that people can find not just the technical resources but support, encouragement, tips and advice from people who have taken on exactly the same issue in their home patch. All of this can be provided without the need for any great organisation or formal structure.

In Altrincham in the UK, three residents have launched their own online campaign to stop developers building a new town centre. Their 'Against Altair' campaign is based on a simple website[19] that makes the

---

[19] www.altairdevelopment.co.uk

case against the council and the developers and has already attracted significant local media coverage and online chat. It's one of millions of such campaigns, and because they are driven by local people with no commercial interest but a new power to express themselves and garner support and coverage in mainstream media, they have to be taken seriously by legislators.

This new ability to find websites, chat rooms, bloggers and Facebook groups dedicated to community-based issues or causes is the new force in politics. In many ways, the people who have most to fear from this 'democratisation of democracy' are not the politicians but the people running NGOs. For many years, NGOs have enjoyed a near-monopoly on campaigning on single issues. They have built up deep technical understanding of the areas in which they operate and, equally importantly, the ways in which pressure can be brought to bear on the decision-making process. They are among the best manipulators of the media agenda, and carry the mantle of 'doing what's right for the world' even when they are conspicuously not. Most also trade very heavily on representing the mandate of their 'members' or 'donors', when in actual fact their members or donors are often very ignorant of the ways in which they operate and are often ruthlessly manipulated into supporting an organisation on the back of some high-profile campaigns.

But most NGOs tend to focus on national or global issues. Where they take on local issues it is often because the issues have a national dimension to them or can be made interesting to national or international media. And most tend to organise and run campaigns of their own rather than facilitate other people's. There is a reason for this: traditionally they have received their funding and their populist legitimacy from their supporters, but unless they show value in this new world, both their funding and (on important local issues at least) their legitimacy are under threat.

They may not be facing the same level of threat as the heads of the NGOs, but politicians have not found the experience of dealing with an empowered consumer an easy one – the crowd can be hostile, contrary and demanding. They do not have to deal with the same threat of physical violence that was faced by their 19th-century forebears, but they still need to develop a thick skin and a calm temperament. As Sarkozy has found, a momentary loss of cool or inappropriate remark can be magnified by the prism of the Internet; bad news cannot be buried, difficult questions cannot be side-stepped. Our political leaders and their campaign managers have also been forced to rethink completely the way that they engage the crowd. No longer can they rely solely on carefully stage-managed appearances in front of a hand-picked selection of their own supporters. They are having to get on their soapboxes – literally or figuratively – and join the often-heated debate. This may not represent the reinvention of democracy, but it is certainly encouraging a new type of behaviour from our political leaders. Politics has suddenly become interesting again.

The Crowd Answers Obama's Call

Technology-enabled citizen participation has already produced ideas driving Obama's campaign and its vision for how technology can help connect government to its citizens and engage citizens in a democracy. Barack Obama will use the most current technological tools available to make government less beholden to special-interest groups and lobbyists and promote citizen participation in government decision-making.
Barack Obama's campaign manifesto 2008

In the closely-fought race for the 2008 Democratic nomination, both Hillary Rodham Clinton and Barack Obama found themselves in a new media arms race. Facebook and YouTube were the new battlegrounds. But only Obama's campaign became described as a 'movement', with its ability to turn online campaigning into real on-the-streets action fundraising and event participation. Partly fuelled by his attractiveness to younger Americans and partly driven by the increasing penetration of broadband and mobile Internet devices like iPhones, Obama attracted a huge online audience. Crucially, he was able to make them do things with the information and materials he gave them.

Hillary Clinton's campaign, despite using nearly as many of the technical toys and employing an army of technology and media gurus, still felt a little more old-style. One example was in the two candidates' use of Twitter, the extremely hip new micro-blogging platform. Twitter allows people to respond from their PC or phone the answer (in 140 characters or fewer) to the question 'What are you doing?' Twitterers fill this space with updates of their everyday thoughts and activities: the profound, profane and, quite frankly, often rather banal. It may be regarded as something of a geek haven, but that was what people were saying about blogging only a few years ago. It is the perfect channel for a politician to keep his or her more avid supporters fed with titbits of information that sound so personal and 'inside', even though everyone knew neither candidate was updating them personally.

Obama, at the height of the nomination campaign in early March 2008, had 14,207 followers on Twitter to Hillary's mere 1,781, but of greater significance was the fact that Obama (or his people) realised it was only polite to 'follow' those that were 'following him'. The Senator from Illinois was clearly not personally spending hours following the electronic updates on the daily movements and ablutions (Twitter is sometimes that direct) of his own supporters – even the energetic Obama doesn't have that much spare time – but what really was being demonstrated was a signal of reciprocity: 'You follow me and I follow you'. And in the more techie or geeky end of the campaign audience, this sort of understanding of new media etiquette is all-important.

In addition to Twitter, Obama deployed just about every social media platform available, which is what you would expect from a man who has recruited Facebook co-founder Chris Hughes as an adviser. His combined total of Facebook and MySpace friends, the new barometer of political virility, numbered 460,000, compared to Clinton's 233,000, although even this achievement was dwarfed by the success of the 'Yes We Can' YouTube video.

Created by Black Eyed Peas frontman, songwriter and producer Will.i.am, and director and film-maker Jesse Dylan (the son of Bob), 'Yes We Can' features celebrities such as Scarlett Johansson and Herbie Hancock singing or reading the words of an Obama campaign speech in New Hampshire. At the height of the campaign for the Democratic nomination, this fusion of music, celebrity, technology and politics was generating more than a million hits a day, making it one of the most popular videos ever uploaded to YouTube.

Crucially, 'Yes We Can' and its follow-up, also created by Will.i.am, 'We Are the Ones', were created entirely independently of the Obama campaign team. In an interview with ABC News, Jesse Dylan said: 'We didn't talk to anybody there. We just came together because it was an inspirational song about change coming out of his speech.' The videos felt like spontaneous and authentic responses of the crowd to Obama's message of 'change', rather than the slick products of the party machine. In a similar way, the YouBama user-generated portal, created by two students from Stanford University, featuring videos of voters giving their personal tributes to Obama, and again outside the direct control of his political machine, proved to be a highly credible and powerful communications tool.

The more formalised elements of Obama's campaign, rather than these spontaneous outpourings from his supporters, also deserve close scrutiny as an object lesson in political crowd surfing. In addition to old-fashioned rhetoric – speeches echoing (deliberately or unconsciously) the activist spirit of the 1960s – he tried consistently to involve the crowd in what he was doing, to give them a sense that his was a shared mission and that they were intrinsically part of it. The 'Yes We Can' chants and direct appeals to supporters to 'answer the call' proved to be highly effective, especially in delivering the youth vote. His share of 18–29 year-old voters in New Hampshire was 51 per cent, in Iowa 57 per cent, in Nevada 59 per cent, and an astonishing 67 per cent in South Carolina.

Obama's success with younger voters has forced every political commentator to recognise the importance of social media as a campaigning tool. A survey by the Pew Research Centre for the People and the Press, which analysed how media was being consumed by Americans during the campaigns for the Republican and Democratic nominations, underlined the significant generational shift that has taken place. Whereas half of respondents over 50 and 49 per cent of 30–49 year olds claimed that they followed the campaign coverage on their local television news, the figure for people under 30 was only 25 per cent. The same survey revealed that 40 per cent of this younger group had watched candidate speeches, interviews, commercials or debates online. Lee Rainie, director for the Pew Internet and American Life Project sees this as an important new phenomenon: 'Young people are particularly galvanised in this campaign, and they have a new set of tools that make it look different from the enthusiasm that greeted other politicians 30 years ago. They read about a news story and then blog about it, or they see a YouTube video and then link to it, or they go to a campaign website, download some phone numbers, and make calls on behalf of a candidate.'[20]

As well as being able to harness the resurgence of youth interest in politics, Obama has also benefited, ironically, from not having the connections or the political machine that Hillary Clinton had at her disposal. This apparent weakness became a strength, not just in the amount he raised (he consistently raised more than she did throughout the whole primary) but in the legitimacy that this seemed to give his campaign or movement. As had been the case with Howard Dean's campaign four years earlier, a few dollars from millions of people seemed so much more democratic than securing millions of dollars from a few people. Political crowd surfing raised more dollars in a matter of months than America's most experienced and polished political fundraising machine had in the preceding couple of years.

Another impressive Obama initiative was the phone bank system that was run from his campaign website. In a matter of a few clicks

[20] Quoted in the *New York Times* (6th April 2008)

online, supporters could volunteer to make calls to people in states that were next up to vote. The system provided them with a suggested script and some phone numbers, and away they went. Compare the effect of being called by an ordinary person (admittedly still a stranger to you) from their home rather than a professional call centre operative. Obviously, friends and family were targeted in this way, but more surprisingly, millions of normal Americans were willing to cold-call other US citizens to get them out to vote. In the days just prior to the primaries in Ohio, Texas, Vermont and Rhode Island, a staggering 2,049,133 such calls were made.

Obama.com also provided supporters with the ability to run their own e-mail or direct contact programs: they could load all of their personal contacts up on the site and then send out standard or customised mailings; they could set up local petitions or campaigns and they could blog from it – and thousands did. Obama's combination of youthful energy and new technology proved an unbeatable combination.

As David Brooks of the *New York Times* put it: 'Barack Obama had a theory. It was that the voters are tired of the partisan paralysis of the past 20 years. The theory was that if Obama could inspire a grassroots movement with a new kind of leadership, he could ride it to the White House and end gridlock in Washington.

'Obama has built his entire campaign on this theory. He's run against negativity and cheap-shot campaigning. He's claimed that there's an "awakening" in this country — people "hungry for a different kind of politics."'[21]

But lest we get all misty-eyed that Obama's use of new technology heralded a complete revolution from the old ways of campaigning, it is important to remember that a huge portion of the money he raised came from old-school tactics like TV advertising — both positive and negative.

Obama also made crowd surfing mistakes, notably during what became known as the 'Bittergate' storm. Obama was addressing a

---

[21] *New York Times* (7th March 2008)

group of supporters at a closed-door fundraiser and made his now-famous observation that 'you go into these small towns in Pennsylvania and, like a lot of small towns in the Midwest, the jobs have been gone now for 25 years and nothing's replaced them . . . And they fell through the Clinton administration, and the Bush administration, and each successive administration has said that somehow these communities are gonna regenerate and they have not.

'And it's not surprising then they get bitter, they cling to guns or religion or antipathy to people who aren't like them or anti-immigrant sentiment or anti-trade sentiment as a way to explain their frustrations.' One of his supporters in the room was Mayhill Fowler, a 61-year-old part-time contributor to OffTheBus.net, which is related to the Huffington Post, the leading liberal blog in the US.

After a delay of a couple of days, she posted his comments on Huffington Post. It recorded 5,000 hits within minutes and over 100,000 by the end of the day. It looked at one stage as if it might derail his campaign. Responding to the critics of her actions, she said: 'We had a fundamental misunderstanding of my priorities. Mine were as a reporter not as a supporter. They thought I would put the role of supporter first.' Her comments underline the blurring of the line between the activist blogger and the citizen journalist.

The lesson for Obama, the consummate crowd surfer in most respects, was that in this new world you are *never* off the record, especially when an amateur journalist lurks in every meeting room. Michael Wolff, media columnist of *Vanity Fair* magazine, is in no doubt about the significance of Bittergate: 'It doesn't matter whose employ she was in or what function she was fulfilling. He said something and was duly recorded. That's the new reality it's useless to ignore. Everybody is going to know what you say. We're going through a transformation process. There is no privacy. You cannot hide.'[22]

The Obama campaign didn't signal the death of the traditional model, but it did show that the old ways were no longer enough in

---

[22] Quoted in *The Observer* (20th April 2008)

themselves and that the secret to re-igniting people's enthusiasm in the political process is to create the means by which they can become involved. For their parents' generation, involvement took the form of the placard-waving political march – against Vietnam, the bomb, or racial or sexual prejudice. To involve this new generation, politicians – and business leaders for that matter – need to follow the lead taken by Obama and be willing to harness the power of social media. It will be fascinating to observe whether the same tactics can win him the hearts and minds of Middle America and take him all the way to the White House.

Chapter 5
New Leadership Skills

Wanted: A president with a complex mind. For as we've learned the hard way, tough issues can rarely be solved with black-and-white thinking. In this world, nothing is that simple.[1]

Robert Kegan, Meehan Professor of Adult Learning, Harvard University Graduate School of Education

To paraphrase Shakespeare's famous line from *Twelfth Night*, some are born crowd surfers, some become crowd surfers and some have crowd surfing thrust upon them. Some business leaders and politicians are natural crowd surfers. They are pragmatic and flexible, without appearing to be weak. They are endlessly fascinated by and curious about human behaviour, and especially that of their customers. They also have the ability to anticipate consumer demands and needs and then respond in the right way and at the right time. Many of the entrepreneurs behind the world's most successful new brands possess these crowd surfing skills. But others have had to train themselves to become crowd surfers, often having been forced to change their behaviour and that of the companies they lead. Michael Dell by his own admission had to learn the hard way, after the blogging community – Jeff Jarvis's 'raging mob with pitchforks' – came close to bringing his business to its knees.

[1] Headline, *USA Today* (13th June 2007)

What type of personality is best suited to becoming a crowd surfer? Writing on the subject of leadership, historian Niall Ferguson has described good leaders as 'the ones that realise (a) I'm fallible, and (b) the world is chaotic'. Echoing the sentiment expressed by Intel's Andrew Grove in his bestselling book *Only the Paranoid Survive*, Ferguson also suggests that 'insecurity is ... an important part of being a good leader. You have to be aware of your vulnerability'.[2] Bill Gates makes a similar point: 'In this business, by the time you realise you're in trouble, it's too late to save yourself. Unless you're running scared all the time, you're gone.'

In his book *I'm No Superman*[3] (which has to be the best title ever for a book on leadership), Professor Santiago Alvarez de Mon of the IESE Business School in Spain argues that if business leaders are to succeed, they must abandon any ambitions to be Superman. He believes that recognising their vulnerability can be a symptom of strength, allowing them to be better able to deal with reality. He also sees humility as a fundamental quality for a successful executive, a quality that allows leaders to avoid getting carried away by short-term success, to rebound after failure, and to be willing to seek help from those around them.

In *The Wisdom of Crowds*, James Surowiecki describes how our faith in the intellectual powers of the CEO is one of the barriers to accepting the collective wisdom of the crowd. He describes the dangers in assuming that 'true intelligence resides only in individuals, so that finding the right person – the right consultant, the right CEO – will make all the difference'. Such an assumption panders to the ego of the arrogant CEO who sees himself or herself as the smartest person in the room and therefore the one best placed to solve every problem. According to management guru Tom Peters: 'In weird, wild textbook-defying times like these, the model of leader as "all-knowing commander and order-giver extraordinaire" is fatally and fundamentally flawed.'[4]

[2] Interviewed in *Business Strategy Review* (Summer 2007)

[3] *No soy supermán*, Santiago Alvarez de Mon (IESE, 2007)

[4] *Leadership*, Tom Peters (Dorling Kindersley, 2005)

One of the most common sentiments expressed by many business leaders today is that things feel out of control. For some this is highly disturbing – it conflicts with their idea that management is all about the imposition of control and the search for predictability and certainty. Trying to find order amidst the chaos is the thing that keeps them awake at night. Sir Martin Sorrell, the head of agency giant WPP, is clearly not one of them: 'These days, complexity goes with the territory. Anybody who believes that life is going to become simpler in this day and age needs to have their head examined. In an increasingly networked world, the 21st century is not for tidy minds. I think – certainly in our business – trying to simplify complexity actually ends up in destroying value; that keeping complexity adds to value.'[5]

Leaders such as Sorrell appear to be the ones most likely to thrive in this new world – they are comfortable with ambiguity and uncertainty, possibly even chaos. Tom Peters, as befitting the author of a book called *Thriving on Chaos*, describes them as leaders who 'love the mess' and defines 'crappy leadership' as 'the leader who needs to be comfortably in control'[6].

Writing about the forthcoming US presidential election, Robert Kegan, Professor of Adult Learning at Harvard University Graduate School of Education and author of *In Over Our Heads: The Mental Demands of Modern Life*, criticises the over-simplistic approach taken by George W Bush to highly complex foreign policy issues. He argues that the problems created in Iraq are largely a product of Bush's simple, homespun view that everything can be seen in terms of black and white, good guys versus bad guys: 'All our lives, we have heard that the world is a dangerous place and indeed it is: but the simple world – especially when this is where the leader lives – is much more dangerous ... In a complex world, a complex mind in a leader is no luxury. We simply cannot afford to do otherwise.'[7]

---

[5] Quoted in *Management Today* (April 2008)

[6] *Leadership*, Tom Peters (Dorling Kindersley, 2005)

[7] *USA Today* (13th June 2007)

Lovers of chaos and complexity are able to fight the natural human instinct to try to impose order on every situation. In fact, according to the authors of one business book, avoiding neatness and embracing a degree of disorganisation can actually be beneficial: 'Though it flies in the face of almost universally accepted wisdom, moderately disorganised people, institutions and systems frequently turn out to be more efficient, more creative, and in general more effective than highly organised ones.'[8] Our children are already using this as an excuse not to tidy their bedrooms.

The authors of *A Perfect Mess* point to the success of Arnold Schwarzenegger, who they describe as being 'a master at looking neat while keeping major aspects of his life steeped in mess' and as someone who has 'overachieved through improvisation and inconsistency'. His laissez-faire management style was demonstrated during his campaign for governor of California: 'Schwarzenegger didn't have a schedule. He refused to make appointments except in unusual circumstances. He lives what he calls "an improvisational lifestyle". It didn't mean you couldn't get to see him: it meant that you called him up, and he was either free to meet you just then or you called back another time. If he did meet you, it might be for five minutes or five hours – he'd see how it went.' It sounds like a nightmare for the people trying to manage his schedule, but it all adds to the image Schwarzenegger likes to present of himself as being cut from a different cloth than the typical politician.

Another actor turned politician, Ronald Reagan, adopted a similarly laid-back approach to the US presidency. He made it very obvious to all that he was not interested in the minutiae of government and more than happy to let the people around him make decisions. His supporters regarded this as a key selling point for their man, with *Time* magazine commenting that 'the phrase "Reagan is not a detail man" is a mantra among Reaganites and suggests that he sees the big picture, that "details" are for smaller minds.'[9] The magazine went on to

---

[8] *A Perfect Mess: The Hidden Benefits of Disorder*, Eric Abrahamson & David H Freedman (Weidenfeld & Nicolson, 2006)

[9] *Time* (8th December 1986)

describe how Reagan's philosophy shaped his approach to the critical negotiations with Gorbachev during the last days of the Cold War: 'In preparation for the Iceland summit, Reagan did not study the history and nuances of America's arms-control strategies; instead he practiced ways to sell Gorbachev on SDI [Strategic Defense Initiative]. To get himself into the right frame of mind, he read Tom Clancy's *Red Storm Rising*, a potboiler about a non-nuclear war between NATO and the Soviet bloc. On a political trip the day before he left for Iceland, Reagan passed his time aboard Air Force One chatting with Secret Service agents. He negotiated with Gorbachev on instinct. His approach could have led to the type of breakthrough that happens only when leaders sweep aside details and discuss the big picture. Or it could have ended hopes for a limited agreement on European missiles and the use of Star Wars as a bargaining tool.' He was as far from a control freak as it is possible to be – an out of control freak?

During the early years of his presidency, Reagan's relaxed, 'big picture' approach – Colin Powell described him as 'a great conceptualiser' – proved immensely popular with the US public, who had grown tired of the micro-management of his predecessor Jimmy Carter, who was described by Steven Roberts in the *New York Times* as being 'obsessed by the tiniest details of government, down to the schedule for the White House tennis court.'[10]

Reagan's political style continues to earn plaudits from today's political leaders. During the campaign for the 2008 Republican nomination, Mitt Romney proclaimed that 'as I get older Ronald Reagan seems to get smarter'. And even the voice of a new political generation, Barack Obama, told a Nevada newspaper that Reagan provided America with 'clarity, optimism and a sense of dynamism'.

He was able to get away with a blatant disregard for the details of politics and a cavalier approach to preparation because of the quality of his inner circle. People such as Chief of Staff James Baker kept the paperwork to a minimum, ensured briefings lasted no more than half

[10] *New York Times* (6th March 1987)

an hour, and prevented some of Reagan's woollier ideas from seeing the light of day, although they weren't always successful in this regard. Reagan once told a group of reporters that trees caused pollution, and during his first meeting with Gorbachev in 1985 he brought up, in all seriousness, the subject of how the two superpowers might work together in the event of an alien invasion. It was a theme he returned to two years later in a speech to the United Nations general assembly, in which he bemused the audience by admitting that 'I occasionally think how our differences worldwide would vanish if we were facing an alien threat from outside this world'.

Ultimately, Reagan's style proved his undoing during the Iran-Contra scandal that clouded his later years in office. The public was shocked by his clear disengagement from the business of government and by his admission that he chose not to know what was going on. Some have suggested that Reagan was already exhibiting signs of the Alzheimer's disease that was to afflict him in his later years and so it would be unfair to criticise him for seeming to be out of touch during the Iran-Contra enquiry. Other, less charitable, commentators believe that he was paying the price for his leadership style: his refusal to get involved in the political detail had finally caught up with him. It will be interesting to observe whether Schwarzenegger can avoid the same mistakes.

The antithesis of the Reagan style was embodied by the man who came to symbolise American business leadership in the late 20th century, Jack Welch. His principles and methods have inspired numerous business books and the near slavish support of academics and business leaders alike. His attention to detail was legendary, although he combined this with informality, which he himself acknowledged in an interview with *BusinessWeek* in 1998: 'The story about GE that hasn't been told is the value of an informal place. I think it is a big thought. I don't think people have ever figured out that being informal is a big deal.'[11]

The magazine described what Welch meant by informality: 'Making the company "informal" means violating the chain of command,

---

[11] *BusinessWeek* (8th June 1998)

communicating across layers, paying people as if they worked not for a big company but for a demanding entrepreneur where nearly everyone knows the boss. It has as much to do with Welch's charisma as it has to do with the less visible rhythms of the company – its meetings and review sessions – and how he uses them to great advantage.

'Welch also understands better than most the value of surprise. Every week, there are unexpected visits to plants and offices, hurriedly scheduled luncheons with managers several layers below him, and countless handwritten notes to GE people that suddenly churn off their fax machines, revealing his bold yet neat handwriting. All of it is meant to lead, guide, and influence the behaviour of a complex organisation.'

Jack Welch would not have had any problem with guiding GE through the age of consumer empowerment. In his book *Straight From the Gut*[12] he describes how 'learning to love change is an unnatural act in any century-old institution'. He expressed his personal view of the leadership challenges posed by major changes, such as the rise of the Internet, in very simple terms: 'You can look at it in one of two ways: as an opportunity or as something to fear. You have to have a certain amount of fear to see the opportunities.'

Welch's genius was in making people working for an industrial giant think and behave as though they were part of a smaller, entrepreneurial unit. This encouraged the development of a fast-moving and flexible culture, capable of embracing change. His highest-profile initiative was probably destroy-your-company-dot-com, in which he forced GE to confront the potential challenges posed by the emerging dotcom business model by establishing dedicated teams who were challenged with creating Web-based business models that could potentially steal business from GE. In this way, he could try to pre-empt any threats from the dotcoms, but more importantly give his people the confidence that GE could respond to the challenge. According to Lee Garbowitz, a GE Corporate Initiatives Group (CIG) manager: 'In the end, they

[12] *Straight from the Gut*, Jack Welch (Warner Books, 2001)

(the GE employees) understood the Internet wasn't a threat: it was an opportunity.'[13]

Welch certainly had very high expectations of the people who worked for him – the nickname 'Neutron Jack' was not given lightly – but those managers who met his exacting standards were given the freedom to run their businesses in their own way. Welch was also a believer in the importance of candour; in fact, he claimed companies had no other option. One of his mantras was 'tell people the truth because they know the truth anyway', which is an important message for many business leaders who continue to believe that they can keep bad news away from the people who work for them.

A collaborative management culture, held together by Welch's obsessive attention to detail and high standards, drove GE forward. Randall S Peterson, London Business School's professor of organisational behaviour, stresses the importance of this type of collaborative mindset: 'Companies are faced with more external uncertainty than ever before. Ever-expanding global competition, fast-paced technologies, erratic economic fluctuations and unpredictable situations have created an increasingly dynamic business environment. To be successful, chief executives and senior management teams must be equipped to cope with unpredictability. This favours the more collaborative approach.'[14]

Typically, female managers tend to be regarded as more collaborative, more capable at consensus-building, and able to focus on a range of issues rather than being obsessed by one particular problem. A study by Cranfield University, using the Myers-Briggs Type Indicator (the long-established methodology to identify psychological differences), showed that male managers consistently came out as 'traditionalists', whereas female managers were significantly more 'intuitive'. The late Anita Roddick, founder of The Body Shop and a global role model for female entrepreneurs, described her personal leadership style: 'I run my company according to feminine principles – principles of caring, making

---

[13] Quoted in *MRO Today* magazine (October 2001)

[14] *Bullies Need Not Apply*, Randall Peterson (*Business Strategy Review*, Summer 2007)

intuitive decisions, not getting hung up on hierarchy, having a sense of work as being part of your life not separate from it, putting your labour where your love is, being responsible to the world in how you use your profits, recognising the bottom line should stay at the bottom.'[15]

Tom Peters is a passionate proponent of the role of female leaders in 'these crazy and chaotic times'. 'We acknowledge that a new fluid world is emerging, but we retain our male-inspired, male-dominated hierarchies. We re-engineer. But our way of thinking . . . indeed our very vocabulary (engineering) continues to be male-inspired. We recognise women's rights but we ignore women's strengths. We value toughness but fail to see that women's brand of toughness is far more steely than men's. We preach the value of a new kind of enterprise but we neglect those who perhaps are more fit to lead it, namely women.[16]

The value of more feminine leadership skills in this new world has yet to be recognised in the boardroom. A recent study of Europe's top 300 companies showed that women occupy just 8.5 per cent of seats in corporate boardrooms, although this figure disguises some wide variations, with women comprising 28.8 per cent of boards in Norwegian companies and only 4.1 per cent in Spain and 1.9 per cent in Italy.[17]

It is surely no coincidence that the traditionally consensus-oriented Scandinavian business culture appears to provide a more supportive environment for female business leaders than the stereotypically macho Latin business culture. This is also reflected in the world of politics. There are more women than men at the top level of politics (i.e. in the cabinet of the ruling party) in Finland and Norway, while the split in Sweden is roughly 50:50. The one country that bucks the trend in Southern Europe is Spain, where Prime Minister Jose Luis Rodriguez Zapatero's cabinet contains more women than men. Zapatero, a self-declared feminist, has also attempted to do something about the lack of representation of women in the higher circles of Spanish business.

[15] Quoted in *Management Focus Issue 12 Summer 1999* (Cranfield School of Management)

[16] *Leadership*, Tom Peters (Dorling Kindersley, 2005)

[17] Source: European Professional Women's Network/Mercer (2007)

He has made equal rights a key element of his first term in office, passing a law making it compulsory for electoral lists and for women to account for at least 40 per cent of the membership of company boards. Predictably, his opposite number in Italy, Silvio Berlusconi, a man not known for his enlightened views when it comes to sexual equality, sees things differently: 'Zapatero has formed a government that is too pink, something that we cannot do in Italy because there is a prevalence of men in politics and it isn't easy to find women who are qualified.'[18]

Without wanting to provide an excuse for chauvinists such as Berlusconi to ignore the skills that women can bring to the boardroom or senior levels of government, it doesn't necessarily follow that 'feminine' leadership styles can only be possessed by women. Writing in the *New York Times* about the battle for the Democratic Party nomination for the 2008 US presidential campaign, Maureen Dowd talked about the paradox that 'the first female candidate for president was rejected by voters drawn to the more feminine style of her male rival ... Hillary was so busy trying to prove she was one of the boys ... that she only belatedly realised that many Democratic and independent voters, especially women, were eager to move from hard-power locker-room tactics to a soft-power sewing-circle approach.'[19]

Meanwhile, Barack Obama – the embodiment of the new man, post-macho leadership style – countered Hillary Clinton's demonstrations of toughness by exhibiting his feminine side: in Dowd's words, he 'tapped into his inner chick'. Her fellow political columnist Ellen Goodman, writing in the *Boston Globe*, described Obama as 'the Oprah candidate. He was the quality-circle man, the uniter-not-divider, the person who believes he can talk to anyone, even our enemies. He finely honed a language usually associated with women's voices.'[20]

Barack Obama's success proves that male leaders can be equally adept at exhibiting stereotypically feminine qualities. University of Wisconsin-Milwaukee political scientist Kathleen Dolan sees him as

---

[18] Speaking to an Italian radio station in April 2008

[19] *New York Times* (24th February 2008)

[20] *Boston Globe* (21st February 2008)

'the embodiment of the gentle, collaborative style without threatening his masculine side', while celebrated author Alice Walker has described Obama as 'someone who honours the feminine values of caring for all'.

Obama is not the only male leader in touch with his feminine side. Look around the business world and you will see other men exhibiting softer, more collaborative, more intuitive behaviours. Howard Schultz, founder of Starbucks, typifies this new style of leadership. US magazine journalist William Meyers describes his style as being 'sensitive, passionate and responsive', and quotes one of Schultz's mantras: 'People aren't interested in how much you know. It's how much you care.' Meyers is clearly a fan of this style of leadership: 'They don't teach caring in business schools, and benevolence isn't usually discussed in corporate management seminars. But these values anchor Schultz's leadership philosophy as he seeks to build connections between people through demonstrations of heart and conscience.'[21]

There is no doubt that Schultz has nurtured an open and collaborative culture within Starbucks. Many profess not to like the coffee or their ubiquitous presence on the world's high streets, but you cannot deny that he has built an incredibly strong sense of belonging within the business. His conversations with employees – or 'partners' in Starbucks-speak – are honest and down to earth. Writing in *BusinessWeek*, Carmine Gallo described what she saw as the reasons for his success: 'His powerful communications skills define a leader who knows not only what he stands for but also the values he promotes, and who knows how to make an emotional connection with his listeners. In fact, Schultz majored in communications in college, took public-speaking courses, and credits much of his ability to win over investors, customers and employees to his communication skills.[22]

He is also not afraid to admit to having made mistakes, another key characteristic of the successful crowd surfer. Originally, Starbucks employed baristas to pull espresso shots by hand. These

[21] *Conscience in a Coffee Cup*, William Meyers, US News (31st Oct 2005)

[22] *BusinessWeek* (5th May 2006)

were subsequently replaced by automated espresso machines. Other changes were also made in the interests of consistency and speed: they stopped grinding fresh beans in front of the customer and used flavour-locked packaging instead. In an internal memo entitled *The Commoditisation of the Starbucks Experience*, Schultz admitted that many of these initiatives had been a mistake: 'I take full responsibility myself, but we desperately need to look into the mirror and realise it's time to get back to the core and make the changes necessary to evoke the heritage, the tradition and the passion that we all have for the true Starbucks experience.'[23] His willingness to admit that he and the business had made mistakes earned Schultz much praise for his candour and honesty.

The challenges posed by consumer empowerment place a premium on leadership skills, although there is no simple formula or style that must be followed. Howard Schultz is a very different personality to Jack Welch, even though both believe that the way to get the best results from the internal crowd is to nurture an informal and collaborative culture. This doesn't mean that they have to adopt Reagan's hands-off approach or share his abhorrence of detail. Most businesses are founded by obsessives: people who spend every waking hour (and occasionally some of their sleeping ones) thinking about the needs of their customers, worrying about maintaining standards. The ones who survive don't abandon their obsessive streak but learn to share the burden; they find collaborators who can support them.

Successful crowd surfers are excited by change. They recognise that the world is a complicated place, but don't try to impose an artificial sense of order upon it. It may intrigue, fascinate and sometimes bemuse them, but they avoid getting too frustrated by its sheer complexity. Pragmatism and flexibility are their watchwords. They listen, they observe, they occasionally surf the tide of popular opinion, but – importantly – they retain the ability to lead.

---

[23] Starbucks internal memo (14th February 2007)

The businesses most affected by this development have been the media owners – the once-powerful newspaper, radio and television barons who used to control the global news agenda. Speaking to the American Society of Newspaper Editors in April 2005, Rupert Murdoch highlighted the challenge facing his industry: 'What is happening right before us is, in short, a revolution in the way young people are accessing news. They don't want to rely on the morning paper for their up-to-date information. They don't want to rely on a God-like figure from above to tell them what's important. And to carry the religion analogy a bit further, they certainly don't want news presented as gospel.'

He could have added that they also don't want to pay for anything. A colleague recently told us that his 20-something younger brother has never paid for a magazine. To a generation which has grown up in a world of free access to information online and free newspapers on the streets, paying for media sounds like a stupid idea. There is a wonderful irony pointed out by media-watchers in the UK that, at a time when media studies degree courses have increased tenfold, the very people attending these courses are unwittingly fuelling the demise of the industry they hope to join by refusing to pay for their own media.

Even beyond the wannabe media studies students, a generation has grown up with the idea that they can become active news reporters, rather than simply passive readers or viewers. Following the bombings in London on 7th July 2005, the BBC received over 1,000 images and mobile clips from the general public, some of which became the defining images from that day. South Korean newspaper *OhMyNews* has taken this idea of what they call 'citizen participatory journalism' to its logical conclusion, relying on its 41,000 citizen journalists to source all of the material for the paper.

The citizen journalist has become a particularly effective foot-soldier tool for the activist movement. The *New York Times* described how a vegan activist, wired with a mini camera, spent six weeks undercover at a slaughterhouse in Southern California in order to expose appalling standards of animal welfare and hygiene. His harrowing video footage,

Leadership and All That Jazz – A Postscript

Our last few days spent working on this book coincided with the death of the British jazz legend and broadcaster, Humphrey Lyttelton. Among the many eulogies that marked his passing was a description of the way he led the members of his jazz band. Humph, as he was affectionately known, played a key role in the revival of traditional (New Orleans) jazz, as opposed to the free-form modern jazz performed by musicians such as Charlie Parker.

By definition, trad is more structured than modern jazz, and trad fans are purists when it comes to the music: Lyttelton himself was almost booed off stage during one concert for daring to include a saxophonist in his line-up. 'Go home you dirty bopper' read one of the banners. Nevertheless, trad can still accommodate improvisation, especially in the hands of an open-minded band leader such as Lyttelton, who encouraged his entourage to express themselves and experiment and improvise around the music, without completely abandoning the musical rhythm demanded by the purists.

He applied a similar approach to his broadcasting career, especially when hosting the long-running 'I'm Sorry I Haven't a Clue' radio panel show, which was built around the spontaneous wit of the panellists. Amidst the comic chaos, Humph was a model of detached calm, keeping the studio audience and comedians in some sort of order, without appearing to impose any control upon them.

As a broadcaster and a bandleader, Humph was a crowd surfer. He had no problem with dealing with empowered people, in fact he actively encouraged them. He maintained an effective and seemingly effortless control over band, comedians and audience alike by surrendering complete control, by trusting the people he worked with and allowing them the freedom to express themselves. Maybe leading a jazz band or a radio show isn't as demanding as running a major corporation or a political party, but we still believe that leaders from beyond the world of show business could learn something from Humph.

Chapter 6
Marketing to the Crowd

> *We've moved from the age of interruption to the age of engagement, from a passive consumer to an active consumer who basically doesn't just sit back and wait for things to be delivered but who goes and seeks things out.*[1]
>
> **John Hegarty**

One of the fundamental principles underpinning this book is that more collaborative or participative forms of communication, which involve the crowd (both internal and external), are likely to be more engaging and therefore more effective. The crowd's participation with a company, a politician or an institution can take many forms: attending a sponsored event, interacting with a website, visiting a brand experience store, sharing a video clip with friends.

We will explore what drives this desire to participate. Why do people make their own ads for Doritos? Contribute to Wikipedia? Share videos espousing Dove's philosophy on feminine beauty? Agree to join Procter & Gamble's consumer panel or take the time to suggest new product ideas to Electrolux?

We will also examine the role of informed individuals in shaping the behaviour of the crowd. How important is it for wannabe crowd surfers to identify and work with these super participants, and what is the best way to capture their attention and harness their enthusiasm? We

actually believe that the answer to this question is deceptively simple: interesting. We will analyse what it is about businesses such as JetBlu Ikea, 42 Below and Innocent that makes them so interesting, and sh how being interesting underpins their commercial success and th ability to involve the crowd.

Finally, we will consider the implications for marketing commu cations agencies. How will they adapt to this new era of participati What type of creative business is best equipped to provide the answers their clients?

The Crowd Demands a Piece of the Action

> *We are developing new ways to be innovative and creative at mass scale . . . The guiding ethos of this new culture, and the forms of self-organisation it is promoting, is participation . . . The point is to take pa to be a player in the action, to have a voice in the conversation . . . Peop do not just want services and goods delivered to them, they also want tools so they can take part, and places in which they can play, share, debate with others. Workers could be instructed, organised in a divisio of labour. Participants will not be led and organised in this way.*
>
> **Charles Leadbeat**

It has never been easier for people to create and share idea widespread availability of what you could describe as 'partic technology' – camera phones, e-mail, superfast broadband conne video-sharing websites – have democratised the creative pro brief glance at YouTube shows that most of the ideas genera not particularly creative or original, but that is not really the The message is that anyone can be a film director, video star reporter, so why not have a go?

---

[1] Quoted in *The Guardian* (11th June 2007)

[2] *We-think: The Power of Mass Creativity*, Charles Leadbeater (Profile Books, 2008)

distributed via the Web, was viewed by millions and forced the local and national authorities to act. The paper was in no doubt about the significance of this type of activist behaviour: 'Empowered by sophisticated hardware like tiny recording devices, and by blogs and social networks, virtually any person now can spread information upward and outward, becoming part of the so-called citizen journalism that has begun to affect policies, laws and even entire economies.'[3]

It would, however, be a mistake to assume that the desire for participation is an entirely new phenomenon. There are few people still working today who can claim to have created a whole industry, but that is Lester Wunderman's claim to eternal fame within the direct marketing community. In his seminal book *Being Direct*[4], which is part autobiography, part guide to the discipline of direct marketing, he describes a speech he gave to MIT in 1967 on the contradiction, as he saw it, 'between people's individual needs and the mass solutions they were still being offered'. He described a market that he believed to be on the verge of dramatic change: 'As I thought about the history of production, selling and advertising, I realised that mass production, mass retailing, mass media and mass advertising constituted only a temporary historical phase.'[5]

The problems Wunderman described and the solutions he proposed over 40 years ago are still valuable for any discussion about why the industry has been forced to change its approach. He talked about how 'we are living in an age of repersonalisation and individualisation. People, products and services are all seeking an individual identity. Taste, desire, ambition and lifestyle have made shopping once again a form of personal expression. Those marketers who ignore the implications of our new individualised information society will be left behind in what may well come to be known as the age of mass production and mass ignorance. Audience participation becomes

[3] *New York Times* (6th April 2008)

[4] Lester Wunderman, *Being Direct: Making Advertising Pay* (DMA, 2004)

[5] As above

absolutely indispensable in our kind of information environment. One of the future aspects of advertising is the custom-made, the tailor-made. Instead of peddling mass-produced commodities, advertising is going to become a personal service of each individual.'

Like most visionaries, Lester Wunderman was way ahead of his time: let us not forget that he was writing during an age when the Internet was merely a sci-fi writer's fantasy. His wise words act as a reminder that the crowd's desire to participate is not simply a response to the availability of new technology.

Human beings are sociable animals, and it is interesting to see how attendances at public events throughout the world are increasing, from football matches to music concerts. A sociologist would probably argue that this willingness to gather in large numbers, mostly alongside a bunch of complete strangers, represents a reaction to the decline of traditional institutions such as the family or organised religion. The crowd is, in effect, our new family, and sporting events, political rallies and rock concerts provide the platforms for the crowd to congregate and the sense of community that we all need.

For many people, this sense of community is reinforced through the brands that they choose to align themselves with. Our relationships with brands may not be as deep and meaningful as those we have with people, but they share many of the same characteristics, especially the desire to belong. Brands play an important role in people's lives by providing both a sense of community that comes from being aligned to a particular group, and a feeling of superiority over the masses. This is, after all, the way that trends start.

They may not feel as though they are part of a group, but the wearers of last winter's must-have item, the North Face jacket, were consciously or unconsciously buying into a shared experience. The trend started with news reporters – every BBC journalist reporting from a frozen battle zone or the chilly wasteland of Downing Street seemed to be wearing one – and they spread quickly to playground mums and commuters. Most of the wearers were unlikely to tackle anything more challenging than the north face of Waitrose, but the jacket was a symbol of their membership of a particular group. They became so ubiquitous that two American girls posted a video on YouTube satirising their friend's slavish devotion to the brand. Watch this space for the North Face backlash.

But simply buying a product and wearing the label isn't enough for some people. Apple fans like the shared experience of hanging out with their fellow devotees – online, in the stores and at events. They feel part of a collective ethos espoused in Apple's 'The Crazy Ones' advertising campaign: a homage to the spirit of rule-breaking and trouble-making (see below). They also enjoy a feeling of superiority over the mere mortals who buy Microsoft or Dell or Sony.

Apple's homage to the Crazy Ones

Here's to the crazy ones. The misfits. The rebels. The trouble-makers. The round pegs in the square holes. The ones who see things differently. They're not fond of rules, and they have no respect for the status quo. You can quote them, disagree with them, glorify or vilify them. But the only thing you can't do is ignore them. Because they change things. They push the human race forward. And while some may see them as the crazy ones, we see genius. Because the people who are crazy enough to think they can change the world, are the ones who do.[6]

Web journalist Jeff Jarvis has coined the term 'social corporation' to describe those businesses such as Apple that go to great lengths to create situations in which they can meet their customers and other stakeholders face to face. Jarvis believes that not enough companies have woken up to the opportunity: 'Most companies I know are not at all social. They live in their own buildings and worlds. Not just people are becoming more social: companies must become more social.'[7]

This is not a new concept. In the early 1990s, General Motors invited 44,000 owners of its Saturn car to a 'homecoming weekend' to visit the factory and have a picnic with the people who made the car. According

---

[6] *Think Different.* Apple commercial, created by TBWA Chiat/Day, Los Angeles (1998)

[7] www.buzzmachine.com (20th January 2008)

to Gerry Moira, chairman and director of creativity at advertising agency Euro RSCG, Saturn didn't want to be just another motor manufacturer; it wanted to be a movement.[8]

Harley-Davidson is another 'social corporation', and its riders share many of the devotional characteristics of Apple fans. It is claimed that the company now makes more money from selling merchandise, holidays and other services to existing owners than it does from selling the bikes themselves, which is hardly surprising when you see the lengths to which it goes to promote the shared experience of being one of the 660,000 members of the Harley Owners Group (HOG): 'The Harley Owners Group is much more than just a motorcycle organisation. It's one million people around the world united by a common passion: making the Harley-Davidson dream a way of life.'[9] Simply owning a Harley isn't enough. You have to show your devotion by wearing the clothing, attending the rallies and hanging out with similarly free-spirited and rebellious types, most of whom revert to being boring old accountants and solicitors when they get back home.

Joe Hice, Harley-Davidson's Director of Corporate Communications, sees the HOGs as the company's greatest marketing asset: 'A lot of those members have sons and daughters who will inherit the passion for Harleys. Others have neighbours and relatives that see them on their Harleys and aspire to be like that. It's really a grassroots network of hundreds of thousands of fanatics out there promoting the brand. Not many products, let alone motorcycles, can claim to have that.[10]

The company claims that the second most popular tattoo in the world (after 'Mum') is the Harley-Davidson logo – which must count as the most extreme form of fan participation. If you walk around the Nike campus in Portland, you will witness similar levels of brand devotion

---

[8] Quoted in *Marketing Week* (14th February 2008)

[9] www.harley-davidson.com

[10] Quoted in brandchannel.com (10th September 2001)

on the legs, arms and torsos of many Nike employees. Marketing the swoosh isn't enough: you have to wear it – for ever.

Fortunately, participation doesn't need to be that extreme. A simple click on the forward button on your e-mail when you receive an amusing or interesting piece of branded content is all it takes to make you a participant. Journalist and social commentator Malcolm Gladwell is an advocate of the power of this form of communication: 'Advertisers spent the better part of the 20th century trying to control and measure and manipulate the spread of information – to count the number of eyes and ears that they could reach with a single message. But the most successful ideas are those that spread and grow because of the customer's relationship with other customers – not the marketer's to the customer.'[11]

Producing material that people are willing to share has become one of the challenges for consumer-facing organisations. In fact, shareability has become the main criteria by which consumers, especially younger groups, judge the quality of creative work. As a focus group attendee, who spoke for most people under 20, told us recently 'If it isn't worth sharing it isn't any good'. This provides a great litmus test for any company: are you creating content that people are willing to share?

In order to pass this test, the content must be surprising, remarkable, provocative and often challenging. This has unleashed an onslaught of viral activity: we've had drumming gorillas, skaters throwing Ray-Bans on to each other's eyes, bears fighting salmon fishermen, surfers creating waves by throwing hand grenades into rivers: in fact, anything that can engage the attention of the receiver of the communication and encourage them to pass it on, especially the bloggers who play such an important role in spreading the word about new material.

This trend has played into the hands of many smaller, creative businesses. It used to be the case that only large corporations with significant media budgets could afford to invest in high-impact

---

[11] Malcolm Gladwell, foreword to *Unleashing the Ideavirus*, Seth Godin (Hyperion, 2001)

television campaigns, the rare advertising campaigns that get people talking. Now the barrier is creative rather than financial, with even the smallest brands capable of mounting high-impact campaigns, so long as they have a good idea. In a typical example, a film created on behalf of US clothing brand Ecko, which appeared to show the US president's Air Force One plane being customised by graffiti artists, was so successful that the Pentagon was forced to issue three denials that it was real. The man behind the stunt, designer and media entrepreneur Marc Ecko, clearly achieved his aim: 'I wanted to do something culturally significant, wanted to create a real pop-culture moment. It's this completely irreverent, over-the-top thing that could really never happen: this five-dollar can of paint putting a pimple on this Goliath.'[12]

The days of the multi-million pound advertising shoot may not be over, but it will become even harder to justify exorbitant budgets on often self-indulgent brand epics when great ideas, filmed on a shoestring, can go global. Traditional media owners and media buying agencies have much to fear from the viral phenomenon. Who needs a multi-million-pound media budget when the crowd is willing to spread a great creative idea virally for nothing?

If you move up the participation hierarchy, the next stage after sharing content is creating content on behalf of your favourite brands, people or institutions. We have already discussed the remarkable effect of Will.i.am's homemade video on the Barack Obama campaign, but what is known as consumer-generated content truly came of age during the 2007 Super Bowl. During the advertising breaks for this traditional creative showcase for the US advertising industry, Doritos, Chevrolet, Alka-Seltzer and the National Football League itself all ran advertising created not by fancy agencies in Madison Avenue but by consumers. Given that the average cost of a 30-second television spot during the Super Bowl can be up to $2.6 million, this demonstrated tremendous faith in the creative abilities of consumers and the power of user-generated content to cut through the advertising clutter.

[12] *Wired* magazine (22nd June 2004)

The fact that one of the Doritos commercials was rated by viewers as their favourite ad suggests that it was a gamble worth taking. Jared Dougherty, a spokesman for Doritos, which ran a national competition to select its Super Bowl ad, sees this as part of a wider consumer trend: 'In today's increasingly reality-driven world, people are looking for new ways to interact with, help shape and even personalise what is important to them. Doritos has had success with star-studded Super Bowl commercials in years past, but this year people want to be in control themselves, and Doritos is giving them that control on one of the world's biggest stages.'[13]

The crowd also likes participating because it makes it feel important, and nothing makes you feel more important than to be asked for your opinion or for your help in solving a problem. Market researchers call this the Hawthorne Effect, after a series of research experiments conducted at General Electric's Hawthorne production plant in Chicago in the 1920s. The researchers, working on behalf of General Electric, noted that when employees were asked to provide opinions about the business, they became more favourable towards the company. Engaging people in research – asking for their opinions – made them feel flattered and privileged, which in turn increased levels of loyalty and advocacy.

Asking consumers for their feedback about products and services creates a similar effect, which is why many businesses have started to use consumer advisory panels. Procter & Gamble has enlisted a veritable army of 600,000 mums to join its Vocalpoint panel. The company provides members of the panel with product news, samples, coupons, and their chance to share their opinions. The panel has given Procter & Gamble advice on all sorts of product and marketing topics: which commercials should be used to promote Herbal Essences, which fashion models should be used in Pantene commercials, and what backing music should be used in a Pringles ad.

[13] Quoted in *Contagious* magazine (June 2007)

Quorn operates a similar scheme, in which 40,000 people provide feedback on new products in return for recipe ideas and special offers. Italian motorcycle brand Ducati communicates, on a regular basis, with an online panel of 160,000 Ducatistas (the most avid Ducati advocates) about new product initiatives. Peter Walshe, Global Account Director at Millward Brown, is a big supporter of these panels: 'The sample they offer is certainly not representative of the typical consumer, but initiatives like Vocalpoint are brilliant for providing rapid feedback from the people whose opinions matter most.'

Some businesses have taken the concept of participation to its logical conclusion, and not only use their customers to provide feedback but to help them develop new products and services or solve problems. This is not exactly a new concept: Alvin Toffler, in his book *The Third Wave*, written in 1980, was already anticipating the emergence of 'prosumers', who would eventually become co-creators, involved in both product design and production. Toffler's predictions required the arrival of the Internet and social software to make them a reality.

Consumer collaboration or crowdsourcing have become vogue terms for this movement, which has spawned Wikipedia, MySpace, YouTube and Linux open-source software. It even has its own bible, *Wikinomics*, to spread the gospel of what its authors, Don Tapscott and Anthony Williams, describe as 'a new art and science of collaboration. Billions of connected individuals can now actively participate in innovation, wealth creation and social development in ways we once only dreamed of. And when these masses of people collaborate, they collectively can advance the arts, culture, science, education, government and the economy in surprising but profitable ways. Companies that engage with these exploding Web-enabled communities are already discovering the true dividends of collective capability and genius.'[14]

The authors of *Wikinomics* allow themselves to get slightly carried away by the historical significance of this new spirit of participation,

[14] *Wikinomics*, Don Tapscott and Anthony Williams (Atlantic Books, 2007)

claiming that: 'for individuals and small producers, this may be the birth of a new era, perhaps even a golden one, on par with the Italian Renaissance or the rise of Athenian democracy'. We may be witnessing a significant new business trend, especially in the area of research and development, but to equate it with the foundation of modern democracy is somewhat ambitious.

This form of co-creation originated with the software industry, which routinely issued prototypes or beta models to the developer community in order to iron out bugs. The adage coined by open-source guru Eric Raymond is a wonderful celebration of the power of collective expertise: 'Given enough eyeballs, all bugs are shallow.'[15]

There is even an open-source beer. Created, predictably, by a bunch of IT students in Denmark, Vores I ('our beer') is brewed from a recipe published under a Creative Commons licence. This means anyone can use the recipe for pleasure or profit. The only catch is that if you make money selling their unique beer, you have to give them credit and publish any changes you make to the recipe under a similar licence.

The students claim that their inspiration wasn't just to get drunk, but 'to see what happens when an open-source structure is applied to a universally known product like beer'. On their website, the students said they are interested in seeing how their beer will get better once it is out in the world, acquiring slight improvements as the recipe is shared. They claim that their ultimate ambition is to create the Linux of beers.

Most of the participation initiatives undertaken by the commercial world fall short of these open-source initiatives and rely, instead, on simple competition mechanics. These tap into the creative talents of what trendwatching.com has described as 'the Global Brain', which combines people who are 'creative and increasingly have access to professional hardware, software and online distribution channels to show (and dictate to) companies what they expect from them, using

---

[15] *The Cathedral and the Bazaar*, an essay by Eric S. Raymond, first presented by the author at the Linux Kongress (27th May 1997)

text, sound, picture and video in ever more powerful ways' with 'the millions of lead users, early adopters, brilliant business professionals dying to give you a piece of their mind'.[16]

Many companies, especially those with a strong design or creative heritage, have looked for support from this Global Brain. Electrolux has challenged design students to imagine household appliances for the year 2020 and healthy eating habits in 2016; Nespresso and illycafe have asked people to suggest innovative ways to serve coffee; IKEA has sought suggestions for storing home media; Peugeot has been able to persuade over 4,000 car design enthusiasts from 87 countries to submit ideas for a new type of car, with the winning design featured in an Xbox motor-racing game.

The crowdsourcing initiative most widely written about was undertaken by Canadian mining company Goldcorp. Inspired by the success of the open-source software movement, the company's CEO Rob McEwan decided to apply similar thinking to the problem of identifying a gold lode at Goldcorp's Red Lake mine in Ontario. He flouted the convention within the usually secretive mining industry and posted all of the company's proprietary geological data about Red Lake on a website. A prize of $575,000 was offered to anyone in the world with good ideas on how to find six million ounces of gold.[17] McEwan's willingness to take such a risk almost certainly reflected his status as something of an outsider in the mining industry: he actually started out working for Merrill Lynch. *Fast Company* magazine's Linda Tischer believes that this gave him a major advantage: 'He wasn't a miner, he didn't think like a miner, and he wasn't constrained by a miner's conventional wisdom.'[18] His different background gave him a fresh perspective on the industry and gave him the confidence to ignore the critics, including many within his own company, who argued that revealing secret data for all to see was tantamount to commercial suicide.

[16] Trendwatching.com (May 2006)

[17] www.goldcorpchallenge.com

[18] *Fast Company* (May 2002)

McEwan's counter-argument was that if he could attract the attention of talented people around the world, he might be able to find a solution to the particular problems Goldcorp faced at the Red Lake mine.

His gamble worked. The Goldcorp Challenge received 1,400 submissions from individuals, corporations, universities and government geological agencies in 50 countries. These identified 110 drilling targets, half of which were new prospects, and from a final shortlist of five targets, four yielded gold. Following the initiative, gold production at the Red Lake mine increased by 900 per cent and costs per ounce dropped by 80 per cent. Not surprisingly, the business media was quick to shower McEwan's Goldcorp with praise. *BusinessWeek* magazine named it one of the 50 most innovative companies, and *Fast Company* magazine named it one of 50 Champions of Innovation.

The Goldcorp Challenge was a one-off initiative designed to solve a particularly difficult problem. In contrast, Procter & Gamble has taken this process a stage further and institutionalised the idea of collaborative R&D under the label of Connect and Develop. Realising that the company would struggle to meet its growth objectives through the existing approach to R&D, Chairman of the Board and Chief Executive Officer, A G Lafley, set the business a challenge: that at least 50 per cent of new products should be derived from ideas generated outside the company. He wasn't intending to replace P&G's 7,500 researchers and support staff, but to increase overall productivity by combining their efforts with the millions of scientists and engineers around the world. In his introduction to the Connect and Develop website, he says: 'External collaboration plays a key role in nearly 50 per cent of P&G's products. We've collaborated with outside partners for generations, but the importance of these alliances has never been greater. Our vision is simple. We want P&G to be known as the company that collaborates – inside and out – better than any other company in the world.'[19]

---

[19] P&G corporate website

Writing in the Harvard Business Review, two of the P&G executives tasked with delivering Lafley's vision, Larry Huston and Nabil Sakkab, describe how 'most companies are still clinging to what we call the invention model, centred on a bricks-and-mortar R&D infrastructure and the idea that their innovation must principally reside within their own four walls. To be sure, these companies are increasingly trying to buttress their labouring R&D departments with acquisitions, alliances, licensing and selective innovation outsourcing. And they're launching Skunk Works, improving collaboration between marketing and R&D, tightening go-to-market criteria, and strengthening product portfolio management.

'But these are incremental changes, bandages on a broken model. Strong words, perhaps, but consider the facts: most mature companies have to create organic growth of between four and six per cent year in, year out. How are they going to do it? For P&G, that's the equivalent of building a $4 billion business this year alone.'[20]

A typical example of a new product innovation delivered by the Connect and Develop initiative is Bounce, the world's first dryer-added fabric softener. P&G acquired the technology underpinning this product from an independent inventor and provided the scale to bring it to the global market. Similarly, Olay skincare products now use pump dispensers originally developed by a European packaging products company. Lafley is suitably evangelical about these types of partnerships: 'I want us to be the absolute best at spotting, developing and leveraging relationships with best-in-class partners in every part of our business. In fact, I want P&G to be a magnet for the best-in-class. The company you most want to work with because you know a partnership with P&G will be more rewarding than any other option available to you.'[21]

---

[20] *Connect and Develop: Inside Procter & Gamble's New Model for Innovation*, Harvard Business Review, Vol. 84, No. 3, March 2006.

[21] Connect & Develop brochure

Huston and Sakkab are frank about the challenges they faced implementing what remains an extremely radical approach to R&D. 'We needed to move the company's attitude from resistance to innovations "not invented here" to enthusiasm for those "proudly found elsewhere". And we needed to change how we defined, and perceived, our R&D organisation: from 7,500 people inside to 7,500 *plus* 1.5 million outside, with a permeable boundary between them.'

The system they created is now considered by marketing consultants and business school academics as the model for product innovation in the 21st century. More than 35 per cent of new P&G products on the market have elements that originated from outside the company, up from about 15 per cent in 2000, and overall R&D productivity has increased by nearly 60 per cent.

P&G's collaborational model will undoubtedly become the norm for all product-oriented corporations. Others have attempted to make a business out of the co-creational movement. InnoCentive, based in Massachusetts in the US, is a Web-based community that matches scientists specialising in innovation to companies looking for help in solving specific R&D problems. Launched in 2001, InnoCentive was initially funded by pharmaceutical company Eli Lilly, who found that, by using what it described as a 'virtual laboratory', it could reduce R&D costs by up to 85 per cent and that the success rate was far higher than relying solely on its internal R&D resources. InnoCentive has subsequently secured $9 million in venture capital funding and is now used by some of the world's largest corporations, including Boeing, Nestlé and Dow Chemical.

Companies send, anonymously, their problems to InnoCentive, and these are then posted on a website that can be accessed by a database of over 145,000 registered scientists from more than 175 countries, 90,000 of whom are based in China. In a sense, this is one of the most perfect expressions of Marshall McLuhan's 'global village'; there are now no geographical or cultural barriers to problem-solving. InnoCentive also appears to be breaking down barriers between scientific disciplines. One of the most interesting findings from an analysis of successes achieved by the 'virtual laboratory' is that the best solutions tend to come from experts not working in that particular scientific area.

Away from the world of advanced science, Dutch website RedesignMe is another expression of the new spirit of creative collaboration. Rather than trying to solve the world's major scientific problems, it concentrates on the improvement of everyday consumer goods. Consumers frustrated by their mobile phone, domestic appliances or other products send their complaints to the website, and other site users can then suggest ways to redesign these products.

The co-creation movement is a high-profile example of one of the benefits of crowd surfing: allowing business leaders to tap into the expertise and creativity of people outside their companies. It is not a substitute for internal R&D – neither P&G nor Eli Lilly rely entirely on the external market – but it clearly benefits them in providing both a fresh perspective and additional resources when they are most needed. It is also unlikely to replace entirely the creative spirit that drives the most successful businesses. The crowd has yet to design a product as brilliantly simple as the iPod, a building as amazing as the Guggenheim in Bilbao or an Oscar-winning movie. It also needs orchestrating, with the systematic approach to collaborative development adopted by P&G and Eli Lilly showing the way forward.

The Science of Participation

The success of any type of social epidemic is heavily dependent on the involvement of people with a particular and rare set of social skills.

Malcolm Gladwell[22]

Researchers at Leeds University have discovered that people apparently behave like sheep. In a series of experiments, volunteers were told to

[22] *The Tipping Point*, Malcolm Gladwell (Little, Brown, 2000)

walk randomly across a large room without talking to each other. A select few were then given detailed instructions about where to walk and the rest quickly followed, forming what the scientists described as a 'self-organising, snake-like structure'. The studies suggest that it only takes five per cent of 'informed individuals' to influence the direction of a crowd of up to 200 people. Professor of Behavioural Ecology Jens Krause, who led the research team, sees strong parallels with animal behaviour, hence the sheep reference. 'We've all been in situations where we get swept along by the crowd, but what's interesting about this research is that our participants ended up making a consensus decision despite the fact that they weren't allowed to talk or gesture to one another. In most cases the participants didn't realise they were being led by others.'[23]

Advertising planner Mark Earls also sees parallels between the behaviour of the crowd and the animal world. He has even written a book called *Herd*, in which he argues that mass behaviour is not driven by a series of individual decisions and behaviours but by a kind of herd instinct: 'We are not a species of independent, self-determining individuals, whatever our brains and our culture tell us. Most of our behaviour is the result of the influence of other people because we are a super-social species – a herd animal, if you like. We are programmed to be together; sociability is our species' key evolutionary strategy. We feel happier with others; our brains develop through interaction with others.'[24]

Earls's favourite example of herd behaviour is the appearance of 'cellotaphs' on Britain's streets. These are cellophane-wrapped floral tributes to people killed in road accidents – the world 'cellotaph' was coined by satirical magazine *Private Eye* to describe these memorials, as a play on the word 'cenotaph', the London monument which is the focus of the UK's Remembrance Day or 'Poppy Day' commemorations.

---

[23] Quoted in the research report produced by the Engineering and Physical Sciences Research Council (14th February 2008)

[24] *Herd: How to Change Mass Behaviour by Harnessing Our True Nature*, Mark Earls (Wiley, 2007)

'Government statistics tell us that in the last 10 years crime has dropped, and yet at the same time every road in every town has been transformed again and again into . . . a "cellotaph". Some of the tributes consist of little more than garage-bought carnations, wrapped in garish cellophane; others are more elaborate.'

Earls traces the roots of this UK phenomenon to the outpouring of communal grief over the death of Diana, Princess of Wales, when a mountain of floral tributes at the gates of her Kensington Palace home became the focus of the nation's feelings – a nation that had hitherto been famously proud of not showing its feelings. According to Earls, he witnessed colleagues who had little or no attachment to the late princess or the royal family making the pilgrimage in order to 'be part of this'. The 'floral fascism' of that time is well recorded, and many people have talked of the pressure they felt under to conform to what they saw as gratuitous sentimentality towards Diana, but which the majority and the national media viewed as a national mood and movement.

Whatever the origins, the fact is that the streets of Britain have become home to floral tributes marking much more prosaic tragedies. These are not 'individual acts' though, according to Earls. 'Nor are they the result of some mass brainwashing by the florist trade or of the garage forecourt marketers. They are an example of the enormous influence each of us has over the others in our lives. Not just those close to us, but those we have never met and never will – people whose behaviour influences other people's behaviour which then in turn influences ours. People like us.'

There have been many studies into the effect of 'informed individuals' on crowd behaviour. These are the people that the rest of us turn to for advice on what to buy, or the people with the widest social networks. Identifying who they are and working out how to harness their enthusiasm and connections are fundamental challenges for the crowd surfer. In *The Tipping Point*, Malcolm Gladwell divides these groups into two distinct categories: the accumulators of knowledge – people he describes as 'information specialists' or 'mavens' – and 'connectors':

those highly connected individuals who are best placed to spread news, gossip and information.

In recruiting mothers to join its Vocalpoint consumer panel, Procter & Gamble concentrates on finding these types of 'connectors'. It claims that their ideal recruit talks to 25 to 30 other women during a typical day, compared to an average of only five. This makes the Vocalpoint panel far from representative of the typical consumer, but they are the people whose opinions carry the most weight in the wider world. The panellists also appear to be pretty enthusiastic about their role: 'Since the time I began as a Vocalpoint mom, I have enjoyed the programme immensely. I mean, who wouldn't love receiving free products, sharing their opinions of new items, being among the first to know about things to come, and let's not forget about all of the great coupons! So, when I received an e-mail a couple months ago asking for a few moms to volunteer to share their experience about being a Vocalpoint member, I thought "Sure, why not?" Imagine my surprise when, about two weeks later, I received a phone call from someone at Vocalpoint asking if it would be okay for them to come to my home and interview me as a possible candidate to speak with a reporter from *BusinessWeek* magazine about my experience as a Vocalpoint member!'[25]

The importance of these highly connected individuals in the new world of social media has interesting implications for the way that companies measure the value of their most important customers. The traditional measures have focused on 'lifetime value': a calculation based on the length of the customer relationships and the frequency and value of their purchases. It is a model based on individual behaviour, treating each person in isolation. What it fails to capture is the value of a customer's social connections. The customer willing to share their opinions with friends and colleagues or post a review of a product or service on a website is highly valuable, possibly even more so than a customer who spends more money, but isn't interested in sharing their opinions.

[25] www.vocalpoint.com/bwl

Researchers claim that it is possible to identify these more socially active and highly connected consumers. At the top of the pyramid in terms of influence are the 'hot' bloggers, capable of attracting large audiences and setting the agenda for the rest of us to follow. Information company Experian has labelled these people as 'super-advocates', suggesting that they 'will have the power to make or break a brand's reputation' and that companies 'use any means to keep these influential figures onside'.[26] Research company Forrester labels them as 'creators', claiming that they account for around 10 per cent of online users in Europe. And these same people will probably be creating and spreading opinion and leading crowds on micro-blogging and social media sites.

They are followed in the socially connected hierarchy by a host of other groups, defined by their level of social interaction online – whether they post comments on blogs, post ratings on product review sites, maintain a profile on a social networking site, or simply view online content generated by other Web users. Elizabeth Fourment is a Franco-American blogger based in Paris. Her 'La Coquette' blog was shortlisted as one of the best personal websites in the 2005 Webby Awards, the leading international award programme for Internet creativity. She is a freelance fashion journalist, and uses her blog to express her views on Parisian fashion, culture and anything else that takes her fancy. For any fashion and beauty brand, Fourment is the embodiment of the socially connected consumer.

Not surprisingly, when French cosmetics brand Lancôme hosted an event in Paris for the most influential bloggers, she was on the invitation list. The two days she spent in the company of Lancôme – being wined and dined in the best restaurants, visiting the flagship store and hanging out with celebrities like Juliette Binoche – provided ample material for her blog. Despite being completely transparent about her motivations for attending – mainly the chance to eat in the best restaurants – her musings on her experience, interspersed with

[26] Experian *Impact of Social Networking in the UK* (January 2008)

references to Lancôme products, will have been followed avidly by the readers of her blog.

Identifying socially connected people such as Elizabeth Fourment is a relatively straightforward exercise. An hour with Google, Technorati or Ice Rocket will be more than sufficient to find every influential blogger or Web columnist. The difficult bit is working out what to do with these people when you have identified them. The people at the top of the socially connected pyramid are almost by definition opinionated, cynical and demanding. They are as far away from being passive receivers of corporate information as it is possible to be. It is rarely as simple as offering them free meals and the chance to hang out with celebrities.

They are also quick to leap on what they consider to be examples of inappropriate corporate behaviour in the online space: company employees joining chat-room debates without revealing who they work for, blogs that appear to have been produced by private individuals but are actually funded and created by corporations. Transparency has always been important for business, but today in the online world it is absolutely vital at all times.

The online community will search out and criticise inconsistent behaviour in a forensic manner. Unilever has rightly attracted much praise for its Dove Campaign for Real Beauty. A series of viral videos, criticising the way that the beauty industry portrays feminine beauty, have been shared by millions of consumers all over the world. It is claimed that one of videos, 'Evolution', has been viewed over 500 million times, despite an initial media spend of only $50,000. In fact, the videos have become so successful that Unilever doesn't even need to spend money on paid-for media to support a new film; consumers are more than happy to do the work for them.

Unilever's confidence in the power of its films to engage the Dove target audience can be seen in its recent decision to launch a Dove-branded Internet TV channel in the US and UK. This is designed, in Unilever's words, to provide a 'unified worldwide digital presence designed to be a trusted source of information, education and inspiration'. The channel, which is typical of a number of initiatives being taken by major brands to develop a Web TV presence, will feature an interactive message board aimed at encouraging Dove consumers to take part in the 'beauty debate'.

The Dove campaigning approach has been given a life beyond the Web, with Unilever creating a 'Self Esteem Fund', which is designed to 'make a real change in the way women and young girls perceive and embrace beauty. We want to help free ourselves and the next generation from beauty stereotypes.'[27] The company has also funded educational initiatives in schools around the world. The Campaign for Real Beauty has substance and integrity. It is not a superficial marketing exercise designed solely to generate a few press headlines; it gives everyone involved with the brand a real sense of purpose.

Unilever owns thousands of brands as well as Dove. One of these happens to be Lynx (known as Axe in many markets). Like Dove, Lynx has been a global phenomenon, becoming a market-leading brand on the back of a series of provocative and often highly amusing campaigns that have engaged its core audience of young males. Many of these campaigns have featured the type of stereotypical beauty images criticised in the Dove campaign: scantily-clad women with unrealistic body shapes, pole dancing, wearing bikinis – you get the picture. This is perhaps not that unusual in a big company where global brand teams tend to spend most of their time working in isolation from each other and pursuing the needs of their own brands.

The crowd, though, does not operate in these silos, and so this behaviour appears to it to be highly inconsistent. The blogging community in particular has leapt on what it considers to be a case of corporate hypocrisy. One of them has even created their own spoof version of one of the more famous Dove films, interspersing Dove and Lynx footage and ending with the line 'Talk to your daughter before Unilever does', which is a simple reworking of the original Dove line 'Talk to your daughter before the beauty industry

[27] Unilever website

does'. Rye Clifton, who was responsible for editing the spoof version, said that he wanted to 'add to the conversation that was already going on online'.

Online journalist Jennifer Whitehead believes that the Unilever debate has important lessons for other corporations: 'The backlash against Unilever's campaign is a salient lesson for big brands using viral marketing to open up dialogue with consumers, highlighting the fact that the same power that spreads the messages that brands want consumers to see can also be harnessed by those who have an alternative point of view.'[28] When a company as smart as Unilever struggles to contain the crowd, it is hardly surprising that many business leaders find consumer empowerment a terrifying prospect.

The principles of focusing on a more socially connected consumer can be applied beyond the world of the Web. 42 Below is one of the world's fastest-growing vodka brands, moving from a few bars in New Zealand to the leading style bars across Asia and North America in only a few years. This progress has not been fuelled by heavyweight advertising. Instead, the team at 42 Below focuses its efforts on the most influential people and places. It enters a new market through the most influential bar in the city. A team of brand ambassadors – typically ex-pat Kiwis passionate about the brand – then sells it to every top bar and restaurant in the targeted area. It also invests heavily in education, under the leadership of the wonderfully titled Vodka Professor, Jacob Briars, who runs 42 Below's global vodka university.

If you want to be taken seriously by the drinks cognoscenti, a crowd surfer needs someone like Jacob: an amazing source of product knowledge, possessed of boundless energy and enthusiasm, and mixer of the wickedest cocktails this side of Auckland. According to 42 Below's founder Geoff Ross, 'Bartenders love our honesty and they love the tone of Jacob, and in return they give us loyalty. They love us for not trying to be corporate salespeople.'

[28] *Brand Republic* (3rd December 2007)

Red Bull is another brand that has built itself primarily through focusing on just one section of the crowd. Launched in 1987, this quirky Austrian energy drink has achieved global sales in excess of $200 million. It has followed a consistent strategy in each market, concentrating on a core audience – Generation Y, and specifically three early-adopter sub-groups: kids into dance music, kids at college and extreme sports enthusiasts – and concentrating on grassroots communication.

Brand ambassadors, recruited from within the different sub-groups, play a critical role. These aren't your typical product samplers. The Red Bull team goes to great lengths to choose the right sort of people: smart, energetic and highly sociable. These are the people on the university campus who organise the social activities of their peer group, the people who discover the new places to go, who try the latest extreme sports, who know which DJs are worth listening to. Here's a typical recruitment ad for Red Bull ambassadors, in this case for the Red Bull Wiiings Team in New Zealand: 'As a team member you will be the face of Red Bull, and your job will be to communicate the benefits and effects of the product directly to our consumers. Sampling missions can include giving athletes a boost at a sports event, giving much-needed wiiings to tired drivers, or energising weary office workers! All of our Wiiings Team members have a few things in common. Do you have boundless energy, passion, intellect and charm? Are you outgoing and a lover of life? Are you professional with great communications skills?'

Most businesses simply wouldn't be prepared to go to these lengths. They wouldn't be willing to devote the time and resources necessary to make it happen. They would take the easy option: throwing out a load of samples and blasting the market with advertising and promotions. Red Bull certainly doesn't take the easy option.

The future belongs to businesses such as Red Bull, 42 Below, Unilever and Procter & Gamble, who strive to understand what drives the crowd and to identify and work with the people and communities who shape its attitudes and behaviour. They don't always get it right – the crowd can be unpredictable and contrary and the people who influence the crowd can be cynical and demanding. But these are the businesses best placed to embrace the new world of consumer empowerment: these are our crowd surfers.

The Art of Being Interesting

> *What's the future of business after the information age? It won't be the latest technology or newest product, but the story behind the product that will provide the competitive edge. The company with the best story wins; consumers will pay for the story that sparks the imagination.*
>
> **Rolf Jensen**[29]

In a *Forbes* magazine article, Seth Godin compared the very different approaches adopted by two airlines in the US: the mighty American Airlines and the small, but always interesting, JetBlue. 'American Airlines might spend $1 million or more on a TV ad campaign and purchase only 100 new first-class customers as a result . . . When JetBlue entered the cut-throat airline business, it didn't do it with clever ads. It installed TVs on the back of every seat and hired the nicest people it could find. The result? The network was activated. Passengers who were attracted by the low price turned into evangelists, eagerly telling everyone not about the fares but about the experience. JetBlue can't control what people say, especially when it gets caught unprepared in the middle of a snowstorm.[30] But it sure influences their conversations by doing things that are remarkable. When David Neeleman, JetBlue's chief executive, responded with a mea culpa, the audience responded. Not everyone

[29] *The Dream Society: How the Coming Shift from Information to Imagination Will Transform Your Business*, Rolf Jensen (McGraw-Hill Education 1999)

[30] This is a reference to a storm on Valentine's Day 2007 that grounded more than 1,000 JetBlue flights. The company responded by offering a 'Passengers' Bill of Rights'.

stuck to the script, but his actions had a huge influence on what people said and how they felt.'[31]

JetBlue's mission to be interesting has extended to the creation of the JetBlue StoryBooth. This provides a facility for customers to record their testimonials and express their loyalty to the brand in front of a video camera. The footage is edited by JetBlue's agency into a series of commercials, viral videos and in-flight films, for a fraction of the cost of a typical airline marketing campaign. Postcards sent by passengers, extolling the virtues of JetBlue, are also reproduced and distributed at airports.

Ikea is another business that is never afraid to be interesting. During the early days of 2008, the IKEA store in New York was brave enough to allow a comedian, Mark Malkoff, to live inside the store for one week and issue a video blog about his experiences. His www.marklivesinikea.com was a brilliant PR coup for IKEA. It worked because they resisted the temptation to interfere, and gave him complete creative control: 'This isn't a commercial for IKEA. They are not paying me to do this. To me, it made sense for my living circumstances and I thought it would make an interesting video. IKEA is giving me 100 per cent creative control of the video content, which is pretty amazing.'

A G Lafley at Procter & Gamble describes his company's version of 'being interesting' as delivering 'pleasant surprises'. 'Hit consumers when they don't expect it and offer a positive solution. It's not about being at all touchpoints, it's about being at the right touchpoint when (the consumer) is open to it.' His favourite example from the Procter & Gamble world is the use of advertising on mirrors in women's washrooms, featuring the message 'Is your lipstick still on?' This was accompanied by a series of five-second television ads with the same message and helped increase sales of its Cover Girl Outlast lipstick by 25 per cent.[32]

---

[31] Your Product, Your Customer (*Forbes* magazine, 5th July 2007)

[32] A G Lafley's speech to the Association of National Advertisers Annual Conference, October 2006

Unilever's Simon Clift believes that the best way to be interesting is to provide entertainment, even if this flies in the face of the traditional view that advertising is first and foremost about selling, rather than entertaining: 'Trying to catch people's attention is obviously harder than ever. The statistics about the fragmentation of audiences, the number of channels and the amount watched and so forth are horrifying. And this has meant that the debate has fundamentally changed. We're no longer having the old argument that says we're here to sell products, we're not here to entertain people. You have to do both, and you don't have a snowflake's chance in hell of selling if you don't engage viewers in the first place. So obviously the next stage is making stuff that people actively want to see and hear.'[33]

Innocent, the UK-based soft drinks manufacturer, has always been interesting. Founded ten years ago by three university mates – Richard Reed, Adam Balon and Jon Wright – with £500 worth of fruit and the desire to create a business they 'could be proud of', Innocent has secured 65 per cent of the UK smoothie market and is close to generating £100 million in turnover. The business has spent hardly any money on conventional advertising – which is mildly ironic when you consider that all three of the founders had spent some time working in advertising. Instead it has generated a sustained stream of positive publicity by always being interesting.

Innocent's launch story is an appealing one for any journalist, and has been repeated in just about every press article written about the business. As Richard Reed recounts: 'Four years ago, we sold our first-ever smoothies at a festival called Jazz on the Green in West London. It was the first time we'd ever tried out our recipes on the public, before we'd ever sold any drinks in the shops, and we set up our stall with a big sign above it saying "Do you think we should give up our jobs to make these smoothies?". Under the sign we put out two bins, one saying "YES" and one saying "NO", for people to throw their empties into. At the end of the weekend the "YES" bin was full, so we went in the next day and resigned.'

---

[33] Interview in *Market Leader* (Winter 2005)

The copywriting on the Innocent smoothie bottles is as funny and engaging as any print ad. You don't call the customer advice line, you call the Innocent team on the Banana Phone and when the calls come in, they are automatically routed to different lines within the business, so you might find yourself speaking to the MD or the boy in the mailroom. Arrive at their suitably quirky offices on a Monday morning and you are likely to find the whole company playing with hula hoops in the car park as part of their weekly exercise session. The company has a strong ethical stance, but manages to retain its sense of fun: one of its highest-profile cause-related programmes featured Innocent bottles wearing tiny woolly hats, in aid of Age Concern's Fight the Freeze campaign. There is even a section on its website for people who are bored, featuring news, downloads, information about the business and its marketing campaigns, described in typical Innocent-speak as 'adverts, posters, pictures and the stuff that we've made'.

Instead of mass advertising, the Innocent team believe that event marketing is more interesting and ultimately more effective in spreading the word about the business and its products. On the UK's hottest weekend on record in August 2003, 40,000 people turned up in London's Regent's Park to Innocent's free festival of 'laid-back jazz, funk, Latin and hip hop'. It was a wonderful example of crowd surfing, or what the Innocent team describe, in suitably homespun terms, as 'making friends'. They created an informal environment for Innocent devotees to socialise and share their love for the brand. People could buy Innocent juices and smoothies from a distinctive 'grass'-covered ice-cream van, with all profits going to a children's holiday charity. The advertising campaign for Fruitstock consisted of three small press ads; word of mouth did the rest.

There is even a scientific definition of the 'interesting stuff' championed by companies such as Innocent: the meme. The term was originally coined by evolutionary biologist Richard Dawkins in *The Selfish Gene*: 'We need a name for the new replicator, a noun that conveys the idea of a unit of cultural transmission, or a unit of imitation ... Examples of memes are tunes, ideas, catch-phrases, clothes fashions ... Just as genes propagate themselves in the gene pool by leaping from body to body via sperm or eggs, so memes propagate themselves in the meme pool by leaping from brain to brain via a process which, in the broad sense, can be called imitation. If a scientist hears or reads about a good idea, he passes it on to his colleagues and students. He mentions it in his articles and in his lectures. If the idea catches on, it can be said to propagate itself, spreading from brain to brain.'[34]

This definition was simplified by Jeremiah Owyang in his Dow Jones White Paper on *Tracking the Influence of Conversation*. He described a meme as 'an idea or discussion that grows and spreads from individual to individual into a lengthy conversation'. Malcolm Gladwell talked about the 'stickiness factor': the specific content of a message that makes it memorable.

Geoff Ross may not talk about memes, but he certainly knows how to produce communication that is memorable. He was also crazy enough to believe that the world was ready for a premium vodka from New Zealand. His 42 Below brand, operating on a shoestring budget, was recently bought by Bacardi for a rumoured NZ$138 million. Dion Nash, 42 Below's International Marketing Manager, has no doubts about why the brand has been so successful: 'We didn't have any money, so the big advertising campaign wasn't an option for us. Even now, apart from a few press ads, we haven't spent much on advertising. It is a bit of a cliché, but not having much money forced us to be creative, to come up with some mad ideas, especially using the power of the Internet to allow consumers to do our marketing for us.'

The team at 42 Below have relied heavily on viral marketing to build the brand, grabbing attention by making fun of everyone from the English to Indian call-centre workers, and especially their fellow New Zealanders. Using simple film and editing technology,

[34] *The Selfish Gene*, Richard Dawkins (Oxford University Press, 1976)

these virals look like they are user-generated, which makes it very easy for people to create their own spoof adverts and thus further enhance the power of the brand. One of their most popular virals, allegedly featuring workers in their Indian call centre miming to a Romanian pop song, took two hours to film and cost only a few hundred dollars.

For 42 Below, the biggest challenge is to stay interesting: to come up with ever-more engaging ideas to maintain the enthusiasm of the crowd. The fact that they loved last year's virals doesn't mean that they will keep on loving the brand. According to Dion Nash, the creative challenge keeps intensifying: 'The people we need to share our viral content are themselves being judged by their peers on the Internet. Their reputations are at stake if they distribute material that isn't good enough. As a spirits company we also have to behave in a socially-responsible way, so simply going for the most outrageous or provocative content is not an option for us.'

It sounds so deceptively simple – 'be interesting' – but these two words should be adopted as a mantra by every wannabe crowd surfer. As with interesting people, interesting companies are the ones that are admired and talked about. Interesting companies have opinions and are not afraid to voice them.

One of the most frequent pieces of advice given by the lifestyle gurus to people who are desperate to be seen as interesting by their friends and colleagues is to be interested. The theory goes that showing an interest in other people's opinions and using their thoughts as a springboard for our own ideas makes us appear more interesting to others. The same principles apply to the world of business. Interesting businesses stay interesting when they retain an instinctive interest in the people they come into contact with: customers, employees, local residents; they listen rather than lecture; they are fascinated by what people think and do. They are also able to institutionalise the need to be interesting. Author and environmental campaigner Paul Hawken has described how: 'Good management is the art of making problems so interesting and their solutions so constructive that everyone wants to get to work and deal with them.'

Procter & Gamble's consumer panel Vocalpoint is the company's window on the world of its consumers and the means by which it knows what they find interesting and how best to interest them in what the company has to offer. Steve Knox, Vocalpoint's CEO, sees this as a highly effective way to engage the interest of a critical audience and cut through the marketing clutter: 'We know that the most powerful form of marketing is an advocacy message from a trusted friend.'

Interesting businesses such as Unilever, Innocent, IKEA, 42 Below and JetBlue keep the crowd engaged and involved by always being interesting. They subscribe to Flaubert's dictum that 'anything becomes interesting if you look at it long enough', and benefit from a virtuous circle in which the more interesting they become, the more likely they are to attract interesting people with interesting ideas, to recruit the most interesting employees, to be written about in the most interesting media and talked about on the most interesting blogs. They save millions of pounds on advertising because they can rely on positive word of mouth to maintain their profile. Now that's interesting.

Implications for Marketing Services Agencies

The agency of the future will have a fine, clear and cultured understanding of some primitive and timeless facts of life. They will understand the nature of choice, the nature of persuasion, and how people construct brands in their heads. Nothing that's happened in the past 50 years has affected these timeless and generic truths.

Jeremy Bullmore, *Campaign* magazine (25th January 2008)

People have been arguing that 'the marketing agency model is broken' for as long as agencies have existed. Type 'agency model broken' into Google and you will generate over 2.5 million results (at the time of writing), most of which feature blogs produced by independent marketing consultants celebrating the death of advertising, the end of the 30-second commercial and the inexorable decline of the agencies that produce them. It always makes for good headlines in the marketing press and makes the consultants feel good about the fact that they no longer inhabit the offices of the doomed agencies: they may not see themselves as rats, but they definitely feel justified in leaving the sinking agency 'ship'.

In fact, marketing services agencies have proven themselves to be remarkably adept at surviving dramatic changes. The arrival of commercial television, the split of creative and media services within advertising agencies, the rise of the Internet have all been accompanied by commentators predicting the end of the agency model, and yet the leading marketing services agency groups continue to thrive. In the past few months all of the major groups – WPP, Omnicom, Publicis, Havas and even Interpublic (which has experienced serious financial difficulties in recent years) – have reported healthy profits.

The people running the major agency groups, people like Sir Martin Sorrell and Maurice Levy, are businessmen: they will follow the money. So if we are to believe the claim by researchers Forrester that, by 2012, US marketers will spend more on social media than they do on online advertising today, then you can be sure that their agencies will become highly skilled at developing social media campaigns. Maurice Levy, the chief executive of Publicis Group, accepts that his business needs to change, but is confident that it can meet the challenge: 'Our role will remain strong, firm, indispensable. All we must do is adapt.'[35] One of his most recent initiatives has been to agree a partnership with Google – the business described by Levy's rival Sorrell as a 'short-term friend and long-term enemy' of the advertising industry. The partnership will include job swaps and the exchange of technological know-how.

---

[35] Speech to International Advertising Association (April 2008)

The major agency groups may be capable of evolving their offer, but where does this leave the traditional advertising creative agency? Many commentators have argued that the emergence of new communications technologies and the growing demand from consumers for more interactivity and involvement in the communications process represent creative challenges that these agencies cannot meet. They are also accused of ignoring the meltdown that has taken place in the world of mass media, remaining wedded to the traditional 30- or 60-second television advertising spot when they should instead be embracing new forms of creativity such as viral communication, word-of-mouth marketing and consumer co-creation. The fact that advertising creative teams continue to be judged, remunerated and headhunted, largely according to the quality of their creative 'reel' (which is inevitably dominated by television work), appears to support the criticism that they are wedded to an out-of-date creative model.

There appear to be two schools of thought within creative agencies: the first argues that the best way to grab the attention of disengaged consumers is to produce highly creative and imaginative visual concepts, using top movie directors and the best post-production facilities, which inevitably means big budgets. John Hegarty believes that, despite the criticism, the 30-second commercial remains a powerful selling tool: 'In a time-poor culture it is the most intense, multi-layered way of telling you about a product. And mass media will always be with us because shared experience is so fundamentally important, a basic human need.'[36]

The advocates of what could be described as the high-impact approach often refer to Apple's 1984 commercial, directed by Ridley Scott, for a record budget at the time of around $800,000. Despite the fact that it was shown only twice – once during the 1984 Super Bowl and once on a small television station in Idaho (so that it would qualify for an advertising awards competition) – it is still talked about by Apple devotees and revered by advertising creatives as an example of 'event

[36] Quoted in *The Independent* (10th October 2005)

advertising', in which the impact more than justified the high investment. Twenty years later, a similar argument must have been used within the corridors of Chanel to justify a budget of $18 million to hire the director and star of Moulin Rouge – Baz Luhrman and Nicole Kidman – to feature in a three-minute film for Chanel Number 5. Depending on your point of view, this was either the most expensive (and possibly most self-indulgent) commercial ever made, or a three-minute piece of Hollywood magic that captured people's attention the world over.

The second school of thought within advertising circles is that in the era of consumer empowerment, the role of the agency should be to either create content that lends itself to re-creation, sharing and parody, or involve consumers right from the start of the creative process. Forrester has described these as 'connected agencies', who have recognised the need to 'shift: from making messages to nurturing consumer connections; from delivering push to creating pull interactions; and from orchestrating campaigns to facilitating conversations.'[37]

You can't imagine Baz Luhrman or Karl Lagerfeld, Chanel's creative guru-in-residence, being comfortable with the idea of re-creation – allowing homemade versions of the Kidman commercial appearing online. How could you place the creative integrity of the brand in the hands of mere amateurs? But other creative people appear to be less precious, often designing rough-and-ready versions of their commercials to encourage consumers to create their own parodies. The highest-profile television commercial in the UK in 2007 was the Cadbury's drumming gorilla, created by Fallon. This simple concept – a man in a gorilla suit miming the drumming sequence in Phil Collins's track 'In the Air Tonight' – was created deliberately to become a viral phenomenon. Fallon's online specialists helped things along by distributing their own spoof versions of the ad and, within weeks, almost 90 different edits, created by consumers, had appeared on YouTube. It was voted advertising campaign of the year by the British public and is credited with generating a 9 per cent increase in sales.

[37] Forrester, *The Connected Agency* (February 2008)

The success of the Doritos campaign, discussed earlier in this book, is also celebrated as an example of the power of co-created advertising. The winning Doritos commercial, voted by viewers as their favourite ad shown during the 2008 Super Bowl, was allegedly produced for a budget of only $50. Doritos' advertising agency, Goodby Silverstein, deserve credit for not only being willing to embrace the idea of co-creation – fighting the temptation to produce their own glossy advertising spot – but also for being smart enough to seed the competition amongst artistic or creative communities. The entries that made the final shortlist were not produced by a complete amateurs but award-winning short-film makers, professional musicians and people already working within the video production industry.

Any decent agency show-reel is now just as likely to feature a Web-based viral campaign or a clever piece of ambient street media as a traditional television spot. And if it doesn't, then their clients should be smart enough to walk away. There is no excuse for any agency head to claim that their agency isn't sure how to leverage social networks or user-generated content on behalf of their clients; they just have to wander down the corridor and talk to the nearest twenty-something employee. One of the great advantages enjoyed by marketing services agencies, certainly compared with most of their clients, is youth. Agencies are young places to work. They say that, in London advertising agencies, when you hit 40 you are faced with two options: consultancy or Cornwall. A cursory glance around London's leading agencies would suggest that there is some truth in this remark. The old ones appear pretty thin on the ground. Advertising, like all other branches of the marketing services industry, has become a young person's game. According to the most recent IPA survey, the average age of people working in creative, full-service and other non-media agencies in the UK is 34, with 43 per cent of employees aged 30 or under. In UK media agencies, the youth factor is even more pronounced: the average age is only 31, and 61 per cent of employees are 30 or under.

The experience deficit in agencies is an issue at a time of complex challenges – and the management consultants have not been slow to fill the skills gap with expensive senior consultants – but if nothing else, the youthfulness of their employees should help ensure that marketing agencies are switched on to the latest media trends. A 25 year old working in an agency has never known a time before mobile phones or the Internet, and the chances are that they will be personally familiar with all that the world of new media has to offer, from the latest social networking sites to mobile gaming. That said, it doesn't necessarily follow that users of new media have to be young: the average age of a computer games player in the US is 33 and the average age of the most frequent games buyers is 38. Similarly, half of all YouTube viewers are over 35. However, new trends are more likely to start with younger members of the agency team. The chances are that by the time a new media channel is being talked about in client and agency boardrooms, it has already been adopted by half the agency.

And if the kids in the agency can't help, the advertising agency heads might be advised to talk to their PR agency counterparts. Public relations has always struggled to be taken seriously in the corridors of marketing power. To marketing heads and senior advertising professionals, PR has been accused of being unsophisticated, lacking strategic and empirical rigour. It feels 'fluffy'. The PR element of a marketing communications programme can also seem pretty insignificant to an agency account director responsible for a multi-million-pound advertising budget.

This is changing. Smart advertising and media agency heads are putting aside their prejudices and applying many of the practices and principles of PR to the way that they plan campaigns. PR people have always been comfortable with the idea that communication cannot be controlled and that, at best, a business can simply influence and shape the communications process. They also value the importance of ideas that can travel – stories that can spread from media channel to media channel, from blog to blog, without the need for expensive media budgets. They have always talked about the power of endorsement by third parties – that the medium and the messenger are as important as the message. In fact, they are already much closer to the Forrester vision of the 'connected agency' – businesses that are capable of 'facilitating interactions and conversations' – than other types of marketing services agency.

Alex Bogusky, chief creative officer of probably the highest-profile creative agency in the US, Crispin Porter Bogusky, is a firm believer in the value of adopting a PR mindset. He no longer asks for rough visuals from his creative teams to illustrate their ideas, but instead asks them to write the press release that might accompany the launch of the campaign idea. He feels that this is the best way for him to judge whether or not the idea has the potential to spread beyond paid-for media: 'I think our way has been to find a really leverageable idea that kind of lives in PR. The original ideas have to be presented as press releases to find how to get really good at that bigger idea that doesn't need media, and then you apply media to it and kaboom! it's even better.'[38]

Russell Davies, founder of the Open Intelligence Agency and a former advertising agency planner, advocates an alternative solution for agencies struggling to come to terms with a world in which the size of the media budget is no longer the be-all and end-all of a creative campaign. When he worked on Honda's 'Power of dreams' campaign in the UK, one of the client's primary objectives was to reduce the amount of money that needed to be spent on paid-for media. In doing so, the agency team was challenged to deliver big ideas that were capable of generating a significant impact without being dependent on high levels of television ratings. He speculated on what could happen if clients decided to eliminate their media budgets entirely: 'What would you do to achieve your marketing goals? Maybe you'd persuade the product and service folks to bake some more brand-oriented ideas into the actual delivery of the product. And swap some of your archive of funny old ads for a bit of broadcast sponsorship. Perhaps you'd talk to the sales people and helpdesk and the delivery drivers: make sure they understand the brand story and are telling it well. Maybe you'd turn your retailers into media channels. Maybe you'd borrow £10,000 from

[38] Interviewed on Creativity-online.com (30th October 2007)

somewhere and do something bold and innovative – because that's all you can really do with £10k.'[39]

Creative maverick David Lubars would also certainly concur with the advice provided by Russell Davies. He is the creative head credited with transforming the approach of one of the biggest agencies in Madison Avenue, BBDO. Lubars was hired by BBDO's president, Andrew Robertson, to help modernise an agency that had become synonymous with big-budget, high-impact television campaigns and was in danger of being left behind by the emergence of digital media.

Inspired by Lubars's willingness to pioneer new creative formats, BBDO has embarked on a frenzy of experimentation. The agency's work for General Electric typifies its new approach, which is far more focused on engaging audiences than delivering big-budget, celebrity-filled mass-media campaigns. In a neat reworking of the iconic General Electric Theater – a half-hour weekly television series that was hosted by a B-movie actor called Ronald Reagan during the 1950s and 1960s – BBDO created 'One-Second Theater'. Specifically designed for the owners of digital video recorders, the One-Second Theater ads contained embedded images squeezed into a one-second frame. These images could only be seen when viewers paused the ad and then watched it on a frame-by-frame basis. The existence of the embedded content was publicised in announcements during TV series sponsored by General Electric, and online.

Writing in *Business 2.0* magazine, Warren Berger describes the Lubars effect: 'At his direction, BBDO began making hip-hop webisodes, pulling funky films off YouTube and turning them into ads, making billboards that responded to text-messaging, and thoroughly confusing New Yorkers by filling their streets with giant office supplies . . . For an ad agency that once accidentally set Michael Jackson's hair on fire while shooting a TV commercial, this was pretty low-key stuff . . . No celebrities, no slick Hollywood direction, no jingles – no sales pitch at

[39] *Campaign* (February 2007)

all. The films looked like shorts at an indie film festival, or something you'd stumble across on YouTube.'[40]

Like Robertson and Lubars at BBDO, Charles Courtier, Chief Executive Officer at media agency Mediaedge:cia (MEC), has led his agency through a successful modernisation programme in response to dramatic changes within the agency marketplace. MEC was voted Global Media Agency of the Year 2006 and 2007 by both *Adweek* and *Advertising Age*, which Courtier sees as a ringing endorsement of a strategy that was devised as far back as 1999: 'The explosive growth in the number of media channels left us with no option other than to change the way we worked. Who can define what is media any more? We had to reinvent ourselves and go to the marketplace with a new story, although persuading 5,000 people in 83 offices to change the way they worked was no easy task. The key for us was in finding a set of words that described what we wanted to deliver for our clients but wouldn't frighten people. We chose 'active engagement' to describe the role we play in actively engaging consumers with our client's brands. It has helped us evolve from a situation where we used to think about media all day to thinking about our client's consumers all day.'

Courtier admits that not every MEC client was convinced about the agency's new direction: 'Some clients questioned our ability to deliver against the promise of active engagement, or were unconvinced by the need for change. And it would be fair to say that we still have work to do, especially at a strategic level and in delivering an integrated offer. Structural silos might suit agency managers but are not what clients need.'

Working out just what it is that clients need has driven agency heads to distraction ever since the marketing services industry was invented. Agencies are programmed instinctively to deliver what they think their clients will buy, and this is where it is possible to detect a degree of hypocrisy in the marketing department. Many marketing heads who

[40] *Business 2.0* magazine (9th May 2007)

talk on conference platforms about the need to embrace new solutions, to think outside the box, are remarkably conservative when it comes to actually commissioning work from their agencies. 'We want you to take risks . . . but not very big ones' is an all-too-familiar refrain. This is also the reason why every award-winning campaign at Cannes or similar marketing festival owes its existence to a client who is willing to allow its agencies to take risks.

The problem facing agency clients is that they are being pulled in two very different directions. On the one hand they are being told that innovation and creativity are more important than ever if they are to respond to intense competition, changing patterns of consumer behaviour and a fragmented media market. On the other, they are under huge pressure from their colleagues in the boardroom to be more accountable in everything that they do. A recent report from the Association of National Advertisers in the US warned that 'dissatisfaction about marketing measurement and internal marketing accountability processes is rampant' and that 'although progress has been made, there is a substantial gap that still needs to be bridged.'[41]

As far as their fellow senior managers are concerned, marketers lack empirical rigour. A report by McKinsey for the Marketing Society in the UK claimed that: 'Marketers are seen to place a premium on the ability to be creative, often being quite dismissive of the analytical and process skills of their colleagues in other departments.'[42] Who said being a client was easy? It doesn't help matters that the average tenure of a Chief Marketing Officer is only just over two years, hardly enough time to understand the challenges they face, let alone win the confidence of their senior colleagues around the board table.

Marketing services agencies have always had to keep up with social, media and technological trends. The challenges posed by consumer empowerment – expressed through the rise of social networks and

[41] ANA (September 2007)

[42] McKinsey's Report for UK Marketing Society (2005)

consumer-generated or customised content – are significant, and what is defined as traditional advertising is likely to continue to decline in importance. However the success of Fallon, BBDO and MEC shows how the smartest agencies – those that understand how to engage the crowd – will continue to thrive.

Chapter 7
Technology to the Rescue

More than a quarter of eight to eleven year olds who are online in the UK have a profile on a social network.

UK Ofcom Report, April 2008

As we admitted in the introduction to this book, neither of us could be accused of being technophiles, but when even Pope Benedict XVI is using text messaging, digital prayer walls and Facebook-style online communities to connect with young Catholics around the world, it is difficult to see how any of us can afford to ignore the ways in which new technology is being harnessed to engage the crowd.

We will start by looking at the CEO blog and analyse the extent to which it is transforming corporate communications by creating a genuine dialogue between the people at the top of an organisation and employees, customers and other stakeholders.

The social media hyperbole has been so intense that we cannot avoid spending some time reviewing the implications of this phenomenon. Every day, millions of people, especially those much-sought-after younger consumers, are having conversations and sharing content through social networks, blogs, wikis, message boards and media-sharing sites. This is where the crowd increasingly hangs out, so it is hardly surprising that companies and politicians have tried to grab a piece of the action. Barack Obama's use of Twitter, Facebook and other social media appears to have been highly effective, especially in overcoming the apathy of younger voters. But the world of social media can also be a very unforgiving place and, so far, most of the social media initiatives undertaken by commercial organisations have proven clumsy and inappropriate.

Finally, we will take a look into the future to see how developments in mobile technology and the convergence of television and online technology can be harnessed by the crowd surfers of the future.

How the CEO Blog is Transforming Corporate Communications

Blogging effectively enables participation in communities you wish to cultivate – employees, partners, the next generation of technology developers and leaders, customers and potential customers, to name but a few ... Through my blog, I am able to immediately and directly reach all of these communities to discuss everything from business and operational priorities to technology developments and company culture.
Jonathan Schwartz, COO of Sun Microsystems

Relatively few CEOs blog in the truest sense of the word. They may issue e-mail missives from on high, but few have shown themselves willing to participate in an open and honest dialogue with the crowd – admitting when things have gone wrong as well as celebrating corporate success. Only 54 (10.8 per cent) of the *Fortune* 500 have company blogs, and few of these are CEO-authored, which is a bit ironic when you consider that the definition of a blog is a *personal* online journal.[1]

This reluctance to blog also has an impact further down the organisational chain. If the person at the top is willing to descend from on high, enter the online community and talk like a real person, it becomes so much easier for other people in the firm to do the same.

[1] *Fortune* 500 Business Blogging Wiki (February 2008)

We have already discussed the challenges faced by any wannabe blogger within Apple, given Steve Jobs's distaste for sharing any news about his business with the wider world.

Companies can, of course, be great crowd-surfing firms without a CEO blogger. Bill Gates never blogged. Michael Dell does not blog. But some CEOs have embraced the opportunity. Bob Lutz, Vice-Chairman of Global Product Development for General Motors, was one of the first senior executives to recognise the value of blogging. In early 2005, along with other senior GM managers, he created the GM Fastlane blog (fastlane.gmblogs.com) to engage in open dialogue and share ideas with customers and potential customers. He is in no doubt about the benefits for GM: 'We've found the blog to be a hugely effective communications tool and a terrific way to conduct a grassroots, largely unfiltered conversation with GM fans and non-fans alike.' He also has important advice for any other senior executives thinking about creating their own blog: 'The key is to leave the corporate-speak behind and keep the tone conversational, open and honest. Anyone who has read our blog sees the real deal, as produced by us and not polished by several layers of trained communications pros.

'Another aspect that helps keep things real is the wealth of comments posted by readers and other bloggers. We don't filter out negative comments, complaints or hate mail. All we do is screen for spam and posts from crackpots using language that most people would find offensive. It's important that we run the bad with the good. We'd take a credibility hit if we posted only rosy compliments, and credibility is the most important attribute a corporate blog can have. Once it's gone, your blog is meaningless. If you filter the negatives out, you don't have a true dialogue, so how can you hope to change anybody's mind about your products or your business?'[2]

Jonathan Schwartz, Chief Operating Officer of Sun Microsystems is another evangelist. 'Sun's goal is to get everyone participating on the network – an era we call the Participation Age. If the Information

[2] *Information Week* (11th July 2005)

Age was passive, the Participation Age is active. One of the great things about writing a blog is the participatory aspect of it, not to mention that it's a great platform to discuss the Participation Age. I frequently meet with customers, and often encounter people who want to discuss topics from my blog. What I find the most compelling is that, through the blog, we are driving conversations that are important to our customers. My blog also generates quite a few comments from readers in different industries, professions and geographies, with each person lending various perspectives that we can learn from. Through the open exchange of ideas and a greater understanding of the communities that participate in the dialogue, Sun will continue to drive its business objectives.'[3]

It could be argued that the head of a company has more important things to do with his or her time than to issue regular electronic bulletins on their various musings to small audiences of online lunatics. Maybe they should leave new media experimentation to more junior staff and instead focus on the grown-up stuff, such as strategy formulation and ordering people around. Unfortunately, by not taking the opportunity to speak directly to people interested in their businesses and listen to what they have to say (even the lunatics), many business leaders are missing out on a big opportunity. The vast majority of their contacts with real people is filtered. In the same way that the political party machine has historically allowed politicians to avoid speaking to real people, the modern corporate affairs department has been good at keeping the CEOs away from real customers.

Some corporations try to address this issue by sending their senior management on to the front line at least once a year – McDonald's managers flip burgers, most retail managers spend time on the shop floor. The corporate blog is another way to achieve a similar objective. It also provides business leaders with an invaluable tutorial in the workings of new media. It is ultimately a more effective way to understand business concepts like viral marketing or crowdsourcing, rather than wait for the *Harvard Business Review* article to appear in three

[3] Interviewed in *Industry Week* (1st August 2006)

years' time. How can you understand the implications of social media on your business if you have never used it? You will recall from one of our earlier chapters the response of one HSBC executive when confronted by a customer protest organised through Facebook: 'We would love to go on Facebook and we have been having a discussion around that, but it is uncharted territory.' Businesses cannot afford uncharted territories when it comes to communication. If some of the senior management team at HSBC had spent some time using Facebook – or at the very least, sat with their children when they used Facebook – they may have avoided being blindsided by this particular issue.

Some commentators have argued that the CEO blog is merely a short-term gimmick, a publicity device designed to generate some positive headlines in the media. And it is true that some of the early CEO bloggers have given up. But most of the early adopters appear to be persevering. They will be reassured to learn that blog readership is already high among opinion-formers in many markets. As the medium becomes more famous for breaking real stories and for covering issues not covered in mainstream media, this growth is set to continue.

More importantly, blogs appear to encourage participation: readers are naturally predisposed to do something with the information once they have read it, although only if the writers avoid the temptation to lapse into the language of the corporate press release. Marketing author Seth Godin is pretty cynical about the ability of most CEOs to avoid this temptation: 'Here's the problem. Blogs work when they are based on candour, urgency, timeliness, pithiness and controversy (maybe utility if you want six). Does this sound like a CEO to you?

'Short and sweet, folks: if you can't be at least four of the five things listed above, please don't bother. People have a choice (4.5 million choices, in fact) and nobody is going to read your blog, link to your blog or quote your blog unless there's something in it for them.

Save the fluff for the annual report.'[4]

---

[4] http://sethgodin.typepad.com/seths_blog/2004/10/beware_the_ceo_.html (26th October 2004)

Even the recently created Blog Council – a group created to help corporate communications professionals better understand how to use this new channel – advises its members to 'speak for a corporation, but never sound "corporate" '.

The one group that is sure to be interested in the views of the CEO is the internal audience. Many CEOs have reported that the most valuable audience for their blogs is their own employees. Not only can they read the thoughts and concerns of the people who run their companies, but by reading the responses from people outside the company, they can get a true sense of how their company is perceived. They may even begin to have some sympathy for the pressures faced by their bosses.

The corporate blog brings people at the top of an organisation into direct contact with the crowd. As is the case with their political counterparts, it requires a new set of skills from most business leaders, and a pretty thick skin to cope with criticism, some of which is bound to be unfair. The adept crowd surfers will find the blog to be an invaluable source of unfiltered feedback on how people perceive their business, and a powerful means of explaining their point of view.

Social Media – Marketing's New Magic Bullet?

It's no longer just about messages that are broadcast out by companies, but increasingly about information that is shared between friends . . . For the last 100 years, media has been pushed out to people, but now marketers are going to be part of the conversation.[5]

Mark Zuckerberg, Facebook founder and chief executive

When Naomi Klein bemoaned the invasion of public spaces by voracious brand owners in her anti-brand polemic *No Logo*, she could have been describing the battles that have taken place within the

---

[5] Quoted in *Brand Republic* (7th November 2007)

world of the social networks. Advertisers cannot resist what appears to them to be a captive audience, so they have not surprisingly got very excited by the social networking phenomenon. Sites such as Facebook, My Space and Bebo and Second Life have attracted millions of avid fans around the world, especially those much-sought-after younger consumers. Where they go, advertisers will inevitably follow, and it appears that they will find a receptive audience when they get there.

In a study by Microsoft Digital Advertising, 73 per cent of social networkers in the UK[6] claimed to have visited a brand's personal space and 16 per cent had some form of dialogue with a brand. Social networkers also appear to be comfortable with the idea of allowing brands to enter their personal space, with 70 per cent saying that they would be prepared to include sponsored content on their personal pages and 10 per cent claiming that they have already branded their space.

Not surprisingly, brands with a strong fanbase tend to generate the greatest level of chatter within social media. According to a report by PR agency Immediate Future, the top 10 brands talked about across the three main social networking sites in the UK – Facebook, Flickr and MySpace – were as follows:

1 Google
2 Yahoo
3 Apple
4 Microsoft
5 Canon
6 Sony
7 Dell
8 eBay
9 Disney
10 Ford

[6] July 2007

The authors of the report have a logical explanation for the preponderance of technology brands in the list: 'Social media uptake is driven by an audience of early adopters. This group are primarily technology enthusiasts with a natural inclination to sharing information and insight.'[7] It is not surprising to see Apple so high on the list. Despite the fact that he goes out of his way to discourage people from talking about his business, even Steve Jobs cannot gag the millions of Apple fans inhabiting the Internet.

People have always discussed their favourite brands and products with friends, family and work colleagues, and shared recommendations. Before the emergence of the social media, the only way that companies could discover what was being said about their brands, or politicians discover the electorate's view of their policies, was within the artificial world of the research study. Now, they can hear what people think – unfiltered, unedited and unconstrained by any pressure to say the right thing.

One of the great ironies in market research is that response rates in general are falling because consumers are less willing to spend their precious time answering a telephone survey or talking to the clipboard-wielding researcher stalking their local high street, but many of these same people appear more than happy to publish, often intimate, information about themselves on social networking sites. Not surprisingly, researchers are spending an increasing amount of time observing what people talk about in Internet chat-rooms and in social networks.

When the marketing agencies working for the Metropolitan Police in London wanted to find out the best way to engage young black males in inner-city London as part of an anti-guns initiative, they found that the most effective source of information came from the social media frequented by this group. None of the usual sources of information at their disposal – standard syndicated research studies, media data – were as useful or enlightening as Facebook and similar sites.

[7] Immediate Future (April 2007)

Social media is also being used, increasingly, to track the effectiveness of marketing campaigns. Unilever has recently begun to track the impact of campaigns for brands such as Dove and Lynx by measuring the extent to which they are being spread and shared through informal networks online, rather than paid-for media. According to Simon Rothon, Unilever's SVP of Global Marketing Services: 'It can be misleading to look at just our paid-for media expenditure, because a lot of the value we get from the digital world is essentially free or almost free.'[8]

The advice to any business that wants to keep in touch with the needs and interests of its customers and keep up to speed with trends within its marketplace is to institutionalise the monitoring of social media. Anyone working for these businesses, especially those in a marketing, sales, research or management role, should be spending at least part of each day reading what is being talked about on blogs, wikis, Web forums and other social networking sites. They should also feel free to enter any debate, as long as they are completely transparent about who they work for.

The one thing that the social network hates, more than anything, is a lack of transparency. The blogosphere can be a famously unforgiving place for anyone who doesn't appear to follow the codes of conduct enforced by the online crowd. PR firm Edelman (and employer of co-author of this book, David Brain) fell foul of the 'always be transparent' rule in the now-infamous 'Wal-Marting Across America' incident. Wal-Mart and Edelman had been locked in a long-running communications battle with the unions and organised labour over working conditions, and created the travel blog Wal-Marting Across America to put across the retailer's side of the argument. The Edelman team failed to declare that they had paid for flights, vehicle hire and fuel for the two people who blogged about their experience of travelling across the United States in their RV (recreational vehicle).

The agency and its client were accused by the blogging community of failing to be entirely open about their direct involvement in the blog

[8] Speaking at the Cannes Lions International Advertising Festival and quoted in *Financial Times* online (25th June 2007)

and for allowing people to assume that it had been produced entirely independently of Wal-Mart. The ensuing online storm was picked up by mainstream media all over the country and then worldwide. Edelman CEO Richard Edelman posted this apology on his own blog: 'For the past several days, I have been listening to the blogging community discuss the cross-country tour that Edelman designed for Working Families for Wal-Mart. I want to acknowledge our error in failing to be transparent about the identity of the two bloggers from the outset. This is 100 per cent our responsibility and our error; not the client's. Let me reiterate our support for the Word-of-Mouth Marketing Association guidelines on transparency, which we helped to write. Our commitment is to openness and engagement because trust is not negotiable, and we are working to be sure that commitment is delivered in all our programmes.'[9]

An increasing number of brands have attempted to create their own sites within the social media environment. Social media is built around conversations – a dialogue between people with shared interests. Occasionally these interests can coalesce successfully around a brand: Coca-Cola, Sony, Dove, Marmite and many others have created successful Facebook pages, largely because they have embraced the interests of an existing loyal fanbase. Other brands have struggled, primarily because they have failed to understand the nature of the medium they are dealing with. They treat social media as simply another communications channel into which they can push their commercial messages.

Seth Godin has been quick to point out the issue: 'The biggest mistake marketers make when they see the power of the consumer network is that they try to control it, own it or manipulate it. This always fails, because the network doesn't care about you and can't be bought. The smartest marketers aim to inspire, not to control . . . The network hates to be controlled. The harder you fight to dominate it, the harder it will fight back.'[10]

---

[9] www.edelman.com/mt/mt-tb.cgi/256

[10] *Your Product, Your Customer* (*Forbes* magazine, 5th July 2007)

Unilever experienced the uncontrollable side of social media during a marketing campaign for its PG Tips brand of tea. As part of a multi-media initiative to resurrect a brand character – a stuffed monkey – the Unilever team created a MySpace page for Mr Monkey. Predictably, the social network decided to have some fun with this character, and the unfortunate Mr Monkey soon made an appearance on www.monkeysuicide.com, a site celebrating (if that is the right word) the different ways in which a monkey can be sacrificed. It was actually a pretty amusing site, and the Unilever people were smart enough not to take any action over it and view it as a compliment to the interest and engagement people had in their brand.

How should companies respond to this type of unauthorised content? We have already seen how attempts to silence bloggers through the threat of legal action have invariably proven counterproductive. Jim Cuene, General Mills' Director of Interactive, admits that his company is still trying to work out the best way to respond to the consumer-generated content on its brands that is appearing on sites such as MySpace: 'It's a huge challenge for us, both in how we respond and in what we say. We've been built for one message, one campaign. We're not well set up for this.'[11]

The owners of social networks have also made some big mistakes in an attempt to derive more revenue from their investments. Facebook broke the first rule of crowd surfing with the creation of 'Facebook Beacon', an advertising platform that allowed brands to pump ads without user consent. A consumer backlash forced the site to rapidly reverse this decision, and the service now includes an opt-in element.

Social media is still in its infancy, especially as a commercial vehicle, although most industry-watchers are predicting dramatic growth, especially once the sites make the necessary improvements to their search and navigation capabilities that will make it easier for companies to target their messages more effectively. This ability to target is critical if companies want to reach a receptive audience within a channel

[11] Speaking at Minnesota Interactive Marketing Association (14th May 2008)

that is the antithesis of mass marketing. Companies will inevitably make mistakes, which is something that can only be expected with any new communications channel. The trick is whether they can learn from their mistakes and also listen to what the users of social media have to say. Gary Koelling, Creative Director/Social Technology at Best Buy in the US, believes that this is crucial: 'Who's gonna teach us how to do this social stuff? Our agencies? I don't think so – it's going to be the customer.' He also offers some simple advice for any business grappling with the challenge of social media: 'You must be willing to try, to do small things. Be authentic and customers will be forgiving.'[12]

Surviving the Future

> I come to this discussion not as an expert with all the answers, but as someone searching for answers to an emerging medium that is not my native language. Like many of you in this room, I'm a digital immigrant. I wasn't weaned on the Web, nor coddled on a computer. Instead, I grew up in a highly centralised world where news and information were tightly controlled by a few editors who deemed (sic) to tell us what we could and should know. My two young daughters, on the other hand, will be digital natives. They'll never know a world without ubiquitous broadband Internet access.
>
> **Rupert Murdoch**[13]

If you want to know what is likely to happen in the future, the best advice is to ignore the futurologists and talk to your children. Today's school-age children have been labelled by media commentators as 'the connected generation'. They have grown up with digital media and are

[12] Speaking at Minnesota Interactive Marketing Association (14th May 2008)

[13] Speech by Rupert Murdoch to the American Society of Newspaper Editors (13th April 2005)

masters of a world in which they will always be more comfortable than their parents.

Observations of children's media behaviour reveal two common traits – active consumption and multi-tasking – both of which will have significant implications for the future of the media industry. It is bizarre that the term 'couch potato' is often associated with children's television viewing. In fact, children are anything but passive when it comes to their consumption of media. As US advertising publication *Ad Age* commented: 'This new generation of kids are not viewers, listeners or readers: they are users.' Years of immersion in computer games and the latest websites have given our children a thirst for interactivity. Not surprisingly, this has made them among the most avid users of the red button to access interactive television services. Text-voting or text-based competitions have also become a staple for most children's television shows.

Today's children are also consummate multi-taskers. They appear able to watch television, play a handheld computer game and read a comic, all at the same time. According to the Keiser Family Foundation, a US-based health information and research charity, over a quarter of 8–18 year olds consume two or more forms of media simultaneously at any given time.[14]

Multi-tasking is, in part, a product of the sheer abundance of child-oriented media. Up until 15 years ago, the majority of children in the UK only had access to four terrestrial channels, which showed children's programmes only during specific time slots: before and after school. Today, according to Ofcom, 63 per cent of family homes have access to digital channels, giving children a choice of over 20 dedicated channels, many of which broadcast throughout the day. And in these homes, 66 per cent of children's viewing is of non-terrestrial channels, compared to 47 per cent of adult viewing. The growth in the number of television channels has been mirrored by a dramatic expansion in access to online content, powered by broadband: 49 per cent of 7–16 year olds had

[14] Keiser Foundation Survey 2003

access to broadband at home in 2005, compared to 24 per cent in 2003.[15] It is hardly surprising that children's bedrooms have been turned into multi-media pods, full of the latest entertainment technology: more than three-quarters of 11–14 year olds have televisions in their bedrooms, most of which are linked to a gaming console.

Children are also at the head of the curve when it comes to embracing mobility. One in four 7–10 year olds owns a mobile phone[16], and much mobile behaviour, from text messaging to the unpleasant trend of 'happy slapping', has originated with the school-age audience. Media owners such as Nickelodeon are already supplying programming to 3G mobiles to satisfy the mobile entertainment needs of their viewers.

Do our media behaviours as children follow us into adulthood? If this is indeed the case, then the best way to predict the media environment in the next decade may be to ignore the predictions of the forecasters and instead observe the way that our children consume media. This is not a universally accepted view, with some commentators arguing that media behaviour adapts with life stage. For example, self-declared media pluralist Richard Eyre believes that multi-tasking, for example, is 'a moment in time, an immaturity that will be ironed out as communities resolve around preferred communications media'[17]. He goes on to say that 'however promiscuous, no one will be juggling media this way beyond a certain age'.

Nevertheless, if we accept the idea that many of these childhood behaviours will be retained into adulthood, the implications for media are profound. The first conclusion is that despite the inexorable rise of digital channels, there will be a place for what the industry defines as traditional media. Watching television remains children's favourite pastime, despite the competing attractions of the Web. Print-based channels can also take some positives from an observation of children's

[15] Childwise Monitor

[16] Quoted by the BBC (January 2005)

[17] Quoted in *Media Week* (7th to 14th November 2006)

behaviour. Book reading among children is actually on the increase thanks, in part, to the J K Rowling effect.

In order to retain the attention of their young audiences, brought up on a diet of YouTube, Bebo, 3G mobile and red-button interactivity, media owners have had to provide ever-more immersive and involving experiences. Television programmes are louder, faster-paced and highly interactive: even some pre-school channels now offer red-button interactivity. Meanwhile, computer games manufacturers are caught in an 'arms race' of technology, competing constantly to deliver the most exciting and exhilarating experiences. This pressure on media owners is unlikely to abate as children enter adulthood. Their commercial survival will depend on the ability to deliver high levels of interactivity and involvement, both in the home and on the move.

There seems implicit in the tone of much mainstream media coverage of technology the idea that we are at a place where technology has now got out of hand or is intruding too much into our lives. There are reams of tedious and repetitive features on the impact of BlackBerry-interrupted weekends on family dynamics and individual mental health, and many seem to take the view that this is a momentary aberration and that all will return to tranquil normality once those troublesome geeks have been put back in their place.

A quick glance through the reports of any of the technology research and analyst houses will tell you that we are at the beginning of something rather than at the end, and that the pace of change will increase and technologies become even more 'intrusive' or 'useful and fun', depending on your perspective. Our children will view much of the debate of the last few years as quaintly as we do now Victorian attitudes to the invention of the train or the telephone, both of which brought with them apocalyptic predictions of the end of civilised life.

In the UK, a 2008 report from communications watchdog Ofcom reported that 49 per cent of those aged between eight and 17 have a profile on a social networking site like Bebo, MySpace or Facebook (this last site is probably only used by them as a way to monitor the first social networking efforts of their parents).[18] 'Social networks are clearly a very important part of people's lives and are having an impact on how people live their lives,' says James Thickett, Director of Market Research at Ofcom. He adds: 'Children's lives are very different from what they were 20 years ago. Social networks are a way of creating a social bond.'[19]

So while it is almost impossible to predict what technologies will appear and win out (we would be fabulously wealthy stock-pickers if that were the case), it is impossible to ignore the fact that the speed of technological change will increase rather than slow. But what will this mean to consumers, and how will they use this new technology to affect their relationships with each other and with companies and organisations?

One of the first outcomes has to be even more intrusion, interaction and conversations between consumers and stakeholders and the organisations those consumers and stakeholders think are important to them (rather than the other way around). One of the drivers of this will be the migration to mobile Internet technologies. Mobile and the Internet are still largely operating as two independent ecosystems, bouncing off one another from time to time, but broadly autonomous and independent. Any other convergence chatter you may hear is nothing compared to the gigantic thud that's going to greet the coming together of the Internet and mobile in the next three years.

Jorma Ollila, Nokia's Chairman and CEO, clearly has a vested interest in this new world: 'Mobility has profoundly changed the everyday lives of people. In the future, mobility will be a part of every aspect of life – a part of leisure as well as business. People will create, share and consume digital information and entertainment, practically wherever and whenever.'[20] Increased mobility and the increased use

---

[18] *Social Networking, a quantitative and qualitative research report into attitudes, behaviours and use* (Ofcom, 2nd April 2008)

[19] Quoted on www.bbc.co.uk/news (2nd April 2008)

[20] Speaking at the Nokia AGM (25th March 2004); www.nokia.com

of mobile forms of communication are indicative of a fundamental shift in behaviour. According to the Future Foundation,[21] the amount of time the average Briton spends on leisure activities outside the home will increase by 31 per cent over the next 15 years. By 2020 people will spend 75 minutes a day eating out or going to the cinema, pubs and clubs compared with 58 minutes now, and there will be a 29 per cent increase in time spent shopping and travelling, up from an average 51 minutes a day to 66 minutes. Consequently, the average time spent eating at home will halve from just over 50 minutes now to 25 in 2020.

Will Harris, also from Nokia, argues that 'the mobile phone is the single biggest technological advancement we will see in our lifetimes. Put simply, mobile phones are agents for change, and that change is overwhelmingly positive. Some technologies have been as popular and widespread and other technologies have encouraged change in specific sectors or niches, but for epoch-making mass adoption and mass improvement, no other technology has so radically improved how people live all over the world since the industrial revolution'.

Harris points to a current sub-group he calls the mobile super-user for clues as to how we will use the mobile differently in the future and how it will impact culture and business: 'Super-users live in a world where they know what their friends are doing on a day-by-day, often hour-by-hour basis . . . for a certain type of people, this ability to be in constant touch draws like-minded people together. Super-users tend to be friends with Super-users. It's not that SMS has changed their point of view, it's just that the ability to be in constant contact is something that unites them.'[22]

SMS or texting is the technology that currently drives Harris's Super-users, and he points to some significant social implications of communicating in this form: 'Consider the following scenario. You exchanged texts with your boss. In the informality of 160 characters,

---

[21] *The shape of things to come* (September 2004)

[22] *Rise of the Mobile Super User*, Will Harris White Paper, October 2007.

your relationship is never going to be same again. The things that traditionally shaped that relationship are gone.' He adds: 'The moment you send someone a text you are engaging with them within the rules of the SMS medium, not the broader rules of society. All the traditions and hierarchies are swept asunder in the need to get your message across in the 160 characters.'

While SMS was, and remains, the most-used mobile application of the Super-user, the ever-faster browsers, using the more and more widely spread 2.5G and 3G mobile phone networks that support them, mean some of the more basic Web tools and applications are already genuinely mobile. Social sites such as Facebook already make applications for personal digital devices such as the BlackBerry which allow users to update their status and which link the new mobile phone photo and video applications to current image- and video-sharing sites people use.

The ability to stream video from your mobile phone to a website is currently niche, but in a very short time will seem as natural as taking pictures with your camera and then downloading them to your PC is now. The launch in 2007 of Apple's iPhone and iTouch, both of which allow the user to surf the net using wi-fi, has brought this world even closer. At the moment, though, the arrival of the full experience of the Internet on the mobile device in your pocket is held back by the technical limitations of bandwidth and the still-patchy coverage of wi-fi (though this is changing fast for those who live in cities, where more and more retailers are offering wi-fi for free, and some entire cities or districts are being switched on).

The fact that the business models of the two worlds are so different is a huge barrier. Mobile phone service providers the world over have a business model that charges users for voice time and for data usage. The Web, however, beyond a usually much smaller monthly access fee, is free. Importing the business model of the Web to mobile would bankrupt mobile service providers almost overnight. If these barriers are overcome, the social and business changes will come even faster. For example, those companies that currently monitor and restrict the use of the Internet by their employees will find it much more difficult to do so when these employees merely have to pull out their mobile phone to get online. The current debates about the impact of Internet use at work in terms of productivity will instantly be made irrelevant, and the corporate cultures that still resist the idea that their employees have digital 'rights' or 'freedom' will find it harder to adapt and to attract the best talent.

The phenomenon of always-on connectedness everywhere, combined with applications that allow us to share and express ourselves through text, voice, picture or video, is technically almost upon us. And given this, the ability and desire of people to interact with companies and organisations either individually or as part of a crowd will increase exponentially. If you already think that customers and stakeholders are becoming troublesomely difficult and intrusive, then you should probably quit the corporate world now, because very few firms and organisations will be able to opt out in the future. Crowd surfing may be something that many in business and politics think is still merely an option at the moment, but this change on its own is probably enough to shatter that illusion.

But it is not the only change on the horizon that will have an impact. Other than the mobile phone, the other device that is on the verge of transformation is the television, and this change too could have a big impact on the crowd. The TV has been the focus of most people's homes pretty much since its inception. Other than the kitchen table or wherever we eat, the classic couch-and-TV combo is still the venue of most family time together, and the idea that for many years TV news, sport, comedy and drama were a kind of social glue is a very well-understood one.

Even though the TV is the place where we come together in the house, it remains a pretty dumb terminal in comparison to the PC. The PC, though, tends to be hidden away in the bedroom or study and is still very much a one-person device. Digital television has long promised to address this deficiency and bring engagement and participation into the living room. Already, 40 per cent of 16–24 year olds in the

UK claim to have interacted with a television commercial,[23] although much of this has involved the use of relatively low-tech mobile text messaging to vote someone out of the Big Brother house or choose the next manufactured superstar on talent shows such as X-Factor. Many advertisers have experimented with red-button interactivity, although the results to date appear inconclusive. While viewers in their millions will happily respond to the instruction to 'press red' to obtain new camera angles during their favourite sports event, comparatively few of them have wanted to interrupt their normal television viewing by pressing the red button during a commercial.

So why has the exciting vision of interactive television not become a reality? Firstly, the different broadcasters, dazzled by dreams of generating incremental revenue from things like shopping, gaming and gambling, developed different platforms, making it hard for advertisers. At the same time, for the television viewer the functionality was poor and slow: in order to transact, users had to link in their phone line, tying up the phone and incurring additional connection charges. However, the most significant barrier was the all-pervasive presence of the Internet, offering greater functionality and a much more immersive and consumer-friendly environment.

Consequently, with a few exceptions – such as Sky TV in the UK, which generates significant revenue from interactive gaming and gambling – the interactive television market has stagnated. Many broadcasters have all but abandoned interactive TV as an advertising vehicle. However, all is not lost. The interactive television experience is set for a renaissance with the arrival of the clumsily-named Internet-protocol television (IPTV) – essentially TV over a broadband connection. Once the barrier of limited broadband speeds is overcome, consumers will have the opportunity to surf TV like they surf the Internet today. This hybrid version of television and the Internet, what the technologists like to describe as 'convergence', will not only allow users to watch what they want when they want, but to include an unlimited supply of additional

[23] Sky (2005)

content. It will be less about lots of channels and more about getting what you want on demand. This is when interactive TV is going to get interesting again.

Devices that link the TV screen to the Internet are also becoming increasingly available. Microsoft's Xbox is one, and this neatly combines online gaming with the ability to record and download programmes. Apple TV similarly allows people to connect to the Internet through the TV, as well as giving us sitting-room access to its core applications like iTunes. Gaming and music are back on the big screen then, and out of their personal hidden ghettos of the portable music device and the PC in the bedroom.

The launch of Nintendo's Wii has shown that devices and applications that do bring people together again in the sitting room can sell well and change habits. Until the launch of Wii, with its easy-to-use handheld controller, gaming seemed to many the preserve of adolescent boys who used it to exercise their enjoyment of violence, horror and juvenile fantasy. Conversely, the Wii seems able to bring families together around a device and an experience that is communal, with games that are much more family-oriented and about simple gaming and fun.

The incredible success of the Wii against two much better established competitors in Xbox and Playstation shows there is a real appetite for technology that brings families together in the old TV-and-couch venue. This could also have interesting implications for the way that family groups interact with companies and other institutions. Purchasing items like holidays probably already involves families clustering around the PC, but these would become much easier if the couch more routinely boasted a remote mouse as well as a TV remote control. Family video conferences at Christmas and holiday time to relatives and friends around the world are one use (again, technically possible now), and imagine the power of a whole family lined up on the couch to complain, online, about a duff service they had all received.

Social media has in many circles stood accused of being, well, not social at all. The Facebook notion of a 'friend', whom we may never meet in person, has been held as another example of the splintering effect of technology on the social fabric, but the TV screen could again allow technology to be seen to be bringing families and groups back together again. The companies, organisations and politicians who can understand and facilitate that will gain huge advantage.

The final technological trend which we believe will be adopted by the crowd in the future will be the move from text as the principal method of communication to a world in which video, still images and sound become equally important. Broadcasting our videos on YouTube, video conferencing via Web services like Skype, photo-sharing on sites like Flickr are all well-established behaviours, but for the most part limited to broadband users. As broadband expands and as video-compression technologies develop, we will be able to enjoy a much more sensory form of communication, expression and community. Given the emotional power of pictures and video, this may well be one of the most challenging aspects of consumer activism in the future.

Crowd surfers do not have to become technology geeks. However, they cannot thrive without an understanding of how technology is likely to shape the behaviour and attitudes of all of their stakeholders. Hopefully they will be able to surround themselves with smart technologists. Failing that, they should spend more time with their children. As educational guru Mark Prensky reminds us, echoing the words of Rupert Murdoch: 'Children are the natives in the digital landscape and we, the adults, are immigrants.'

Chapter 8
Final Thoughts

The decision to write *Crowd Surfing* began with a drunken conversation in a bar about why it was that nobody had written a considered and – ironically, given the circumstances – sober analysis of the consequences of consumer empowerment. Everyone appeared to accept the reality that the balance of power between institutions and the public had shifted and that the 'command and control' model of business was no longer relevant, but what did this empowerment trend really mean for companies and other institutions? Was it truly the end of business and politics as we knew it, which was certainly the view of many of the more excitable social media evangelists?

The historian A J P Taylor, when asked what motivated him to write, said that he wrote so he knew what to think. And the act of writing this book has certainly helped us better understand what is happening within the business and political world. We have also been fortunate in having close access to some of the world's largest corporations and to people involved in political campaigns on both sides of the Atlantic.

The experience of Sebastian Coe and his colleagues on the London 2012 team, when facing the wrath of the public over something as simple as a logo, struck us as being a perfect illustration of how the world, at least from the point of view of many business and political leaders, seemed to be out of control. It was relatively easy to find many other examples of how ordinary members of the public and activist groups appeared to be gaining in confidence and power. The lone protester, with a camera phone, access to the Internet and a grievance, now appears capable of forcing even the world's most powerful corporations to make very public apologies and reverse unpopular policies.

Companies that have tried to hold back the tide of consumer empowerment through the threat of legal action have been almost entirely unsuccessful. They would almost certainly benefit from observing how McDonald's has progressed from fighting activists in the courtroom to becoming one of the most enlightened businesses when it comes to dealing with criticism. They should also remember the wise words of Jeff Jarvis and learn to 'love the customer who hates you'. Jeff has been probably the most-quoted person in this book. Not only does he produce pithy soundbites, but he also has the ability to see the business world from the viewpoint of the consumer. His Dell Hell experience has been much written about, but we still feel that the case study is a valuable one, not least because of Michael Dell's willingness to be completely frank about the difficulties Dell faced in institutionalising a new culture of openness and collaboration.

We were fascinated by the different philosophies of Microsoft and Apple when it comes to dealing with social media. Microsoft's ability to accommodate over 5,000 employee bloggers and to work with someone as idiosyncratic as cartoonist Hugh Macleod – the man responsible for the Blue Monster – is incredible for a company of its size. By contrast, Apple is an enigma – a business with a rebellious, freewheeling persona, run by a brilliant control freak. We have to admit that we probably spent more time debating Apple than any other business. It continues to succeed, despite its refusal to embrace many of the most common forms of consumer empowerment – blogs, customer collaboration and the rest. A *Wired* magazine headline 'How Apple got everything right by doing everything wrong'[1] seems to us to be the perfect expression of how the company appears to play by a different set of rules. We decided in the end that Apple was the exception that proved the rule: the product of a particular set of circumstances and a unique leader. If more companies such as Apple emerge, capable of

[1] *Wired* magazine (18th March 2008)

ignoring consumer empowerment and still thriving commercially, we might be forced to revise this view and probably write a new book.

Although it is a truism that a company's most important audience is its internal one, we felt that most of the material written about consumer empowerment has ignored the internal dimension. The Pfizer case study was particularly interesting because of the sheer value of the human capital working in the pharmaceutical industry. Companies such as Pfizer invest tens of thousands of pounds on training their scientists and research specialists, which makes employee retention absolutely critical. Not surprisingly, being people of a scientific inclination, the Pfizer team looked to a technological solution. The results were highly impressive, and demonstrate how effectively social media technology can be used to reinvigorate internal communications. The employee suggestion box may now finally be put back in the store cupboard.

When writing the book we found ourselves drawn increasingly to the battle between Clinton and Obama for the Democratic Party's nomination for the 2008 presidential campaign. Obama's ability to connect with a new generation of American voters, partly through the use of new media, and his skill in convincing people that they were part of a movement for change, seemed to us like the perfect example of crowd surfing in action. We don't know whether this will take him all the way to the White House – the challenge of mobilising the crowd occupying middle America may be insurmountable – but Obama, like Cameron and Sarkozy in Europe, seems perfectly suited to the era of interactive or two-way politics, which is actually a throwback to an earlier era of robust political debate.

Political parties, generally, appear to be ahead of businesses when it comes to embracing consumer empowerment. Maybe the challenge of mobilising an apathetic electorate has galvanised them into action – they have been forced to get on to their virtual soapboxes. Some politicians have not found this easy – Gordon Brown for one is rarely at his best in front of a hostile crowd, where a thick skin and a calm temperament are required. Many business leaders have also struggled to respond to the new climate, which requires them, in the words of historian Niall Fergusson, to accept that they are 'fallible' and that 'the world is chaotic'. For many of them, the idea of management is to impose control and search for predictability and certainty. By contrast, crowd surfers are excited and invigorated by this state of affairs.

We believe that crowd surfing is more about an attitude or a state of mind than a set of rules. We have therefore avoided trying to make this book a 'how to' business manual, complete with 'ten rules for crowd surfers' and the type of process charts and flow diagrams loved by management consultants. We think that learning from the experiences of businesses and politicians is far more useful. There is not one single way to crowd surf – it requires pragmatism and flexibility and a willingness to learn from mistakes. Even the most capable marketing teams can occasionally come unstuck.

As we hope we have shown, there are plenty of excellent case studies available on the use of viral marketing, user-generated content, consumer advisory panels, product collaboration and other forms of customer or employee participation. We also hope that readers of this book will join the debate and tell us what they think. In the true spirit of crowd surfing, we have set up a blog on www.crowdsurfing.net.

'You can't stop the waves, but you can learn to surf.'
Jon Kabat-Zinn

Index